WILLIAMS-SONOMA

SAUCE

RECIPES AND TEXT

BRIGIT L. BINNS

GENERAL EDITOR

CHUCK WILLIAMS

PHOTOGRAPHS

SHERI GIBLIN

SIMON & SCHUSTER • **SOURCE**

NEW YORK • LONDON • TORONTO • SYDNEY • SINGAPORE

CONTENTS

PASTA SAUCES

SALSAS, PURÉES, AND RELISHES

DESSERT SAUCES

INTRODUCTION

When I first encountered authentic French cooking decades ago, I was intrigued by the classic emulsion sauces, such as hollandaise and bordelaise. Their smooth textures and nuanced flavors added a subtle richness to so many dishes. Today, we still come back time and again to these traditional European recipes, but also embrace a wide variety of sauces from around the world, from Moroccan *charmoula* to Thai peanut sauce. In some cases, it is impossible to separate a sauce from the dish itself, as with spicy Indian lamb curry or a hearty Mexican chicken mole, flavored with chocolate and nuts. Other versatile sauces, such as Cuban *mojo*, can function as a savory marinade, a table sauce, or a dip.

Whether you are looking for easy vinaigrettes and salsas, elegant French emulsions, simple and hearty pan sauces, or decadent sauces for dessert, this cookbook will provide a wealth of ideas for every occasion. And the step-by-step instructions will help the novice sauce maker to cook with success. Just as the clothes make the man, the sauce can most certainly make the dish.

Chuck Williams

THE CLASSICS

Grilled ribs with barbecue sauce, asparagus with hollandaise—the sauce is often the most important part of a dish. Although some of the best-known classic sauces, such as béarnaise and duxelles, come from French cuisine, many others—mole from Mexico, curry from India—hail from other national kitchens.

ARTICHOKES WITH BÉARNAISE SAUCE

EMULSIFYING TIPS

In classic French emulsions such as béarnaise and hollandaise, the goal is to force two normally incompatible liquids together. When making either of the two sauces, the temperature of the egg yolks is key: If the yolks get too hot, their proteins, rather than smoothly binding the mixture, will form lumps, resulting in a curdled sauce. You can prevent this from happening by occasionally moving the sauce off the heat, or by adding an ice cube, which will halt the curdling action. For more on emulsifying, see page 108.

Bring a large saucepan two-thirds full of water to a boil over high heat. Add 1 tablespoon kosher salt and the lemon wedges. While the water is heating, trim the artichokes: Working with 1 artichoke at a time, pull off the tough outer leaves and trim the stem flush with the bottom. Cut off the top one-third of the artichoke; then, using kitchen shears, trim off any remaining sharp leaf tips. Add the artichokes to the water and partially cover the pan. Reduce the heat to medium-high and cook until a sharp knife easily penetrates the base of an artichoke, 45–50 minutes.

When the artichokes are close to being done, make the sauce: In a small, heavy saucepan, combine the shallot, tarragon stems, and vinegar. Bring to a simmer over medium-low heat and cook until reduced to about 1 tablespoon, 4–5 minutes. Remove the mixture from the heat, let stand for 5 minutes, and then discard the tarragon stems. Whisk in the egg yolks, return the pan to low heat, and cook, whisking constantly, until the mixture begins to thicken *(left)*, 2–4 minutes. Remove from the heat and whisk in the butter 1 tablespoon at a time, whisking in thoroughly before adding more. After the first few tablespoons of butter have been incorporated, return to the heat and add the rest more quickly. When all the butter has been added and the sauce is smooth and glossy, remove from the heat again and whisk in ¼ teaspoon salt, ⅛ teaspoon white pepper, the Worcestershire sauce, the lemon juice, and the minced tarragon. Adjust the seasoning with salt and white pepper. Serve within 5 minutes, or cover and keep warm for up to 30 minutes in the top of a double boiler over hot, but not simmering, water.

When the artichokes are ready, remove from the pan and let them cool upside down for about 15 minutes. Place on plates next to a bowl of the sauce for dipping.

MAKES 4 SERVINGS

Kosher salt

1 lemon, cut into wedges

4 large artichokes

FOR THE SAUCE:

1 small shallot, minced

3 small fresh tarragon sprigs, leaves minced and stems reserved

½ cup (4 fl oz/125 ml) white wine vinegar

3 large egg yolks

¾ cup (6 oz/185 g) unsalted butter, melted and kept warm

Salt and freshly ground white pepper

⅛ teaspoon Worcestershire sauce

1½ tablespoons fresh lemon juice

ASPARAGUS WITH HOLLANDAISE SAUCE

1 lb (500 g) asparagus

Kosher salt

FOR THE SAUCE:

3 large egg yolks

Salt and freshly ground
white pepper

1 ice cube, if needed

½ cup (4 oz / 125 g)
unsalted butter, melted
and kept warm

2–3 teaspoons fresh
lemon juice, or to taste

Cut or break off the woody ends of the asparagus (page 114). Bring a large saucepan three-fourths full of water to a boil over high heat. Add 1 tablespoon kosher salt and the asparagus, and cook, uncovered, until the bases of the stalks are tender when pierced with a knife, 6–7 minutes. Transfer to paper towels to drain.

To make the sauce, in a small, heavy saucepan, combine 3 tablespoons water, the egg yolks, and ¼ teaspoon salt. Cook over low heat, whisking constantly, until the mixture is foamy, 1–2 minutes. (Keep the whisk down in the liquid, rather than lifting it up; you want the bubbles to be small.) Continue whisking constantly until the mixture is pale yellow and begins to thicken, 1–3 minutes longer. Once it has thickened, do not heat it too quickly or it will curdle. If it appears granular, quickly remove it from the heat, drop in the ice cube, and whisk it in thoroughly. When the mixture is smooth with a glossy sheen, return the pan to the heat.

As soon as you begin to see the bottom of the pan as you whisk, remove from the heat. Whisk in the butter 1 tablespoon at a time, whisking in thoroughly before adding more. Whisk in 2 teaspoons lemon juice and taste. You should be able to taste the lemon, but the sauce should not be sour. Add more lemon juice a drop or two at a time, if necessary. Season to taste with salt and white pepper. Serve within 5 minutes, or cover and keep warm for up to 30 minutes in the top of a double boiler over hot, but not simmering, water.

To serve, transfer the asparagus to a warmed platter and spoon a generous amount of the hollandaise over the tips. Serve at once.

Note: This recipe contains partially cooked eggs. For more details, see page 115.

MAKES 4–6 SERVINGS

HOLLANDAISE VARIATIONS

Hollandaise can be varied with the addition of herbs or other ingredients. For orange-chive hollandaise, stir 1 teaspoon grated orange zest and 1 tablespoon snipped chives into the finished sauce. For tomato-lime hollandaise, use fresh lime juice in place of the lemon juice, and stir 2 tablespoons finely diced, peeled tomato (page 62) into the finished sauce. For mousseline, whip ½ cup (4 fl oz / 125 ml) heavy (double) cream to firm peaks, then fold into the warm hollandaise just before serving.

VEAL CHOPS WITH DUXELLES SAUCE

Pat the veal chops dry with paper towels. Rub both sides of the chops with the olive oil and let stand at room temperature for 1 hour. Preheat the oven to 350°F (180°C).

To make the sauce, first prepare the beurre manié *(left)*. Then, in a large, heavy frying pan over medium heat, melt the butter. When it is just starting to brown, add the onion, shallot, and mushrooms and sauté, stirring frequently, until lightly golden, about 6 minutes. (After 1–2 minutes, the mushrooms will release their liquid; continue to sauté until the moisture evaporates and the mixture is crumbly.) Add the wine and cook, stirring, until it evaporates, 2–3 minutes. Add the consommé, tomato purée, ¾ teaspoon salt, ¼ teaspoon pepper, and the nutmeg and cook, stirring constantly, for about 3 minutes longer. Whisk in half of the beurre manié and simmer until the sauce thickens, about 2 minutes. If a thicker sauce is desired, whisk in the remaining beurre manié and simmer for 2 minutes longer. Remove the pan from the heat, cover, and let stand for up to 30 minutes.

To cook the chops, set 2 large ovenproof frying pans over high heat (if you do not have 2 large pans, cook the chops in 2 batches). Season one side of the chops generously with salt and pepper. When the pans are very hot, place 2 chops, seasoned side down, in each pan and cook, without moving them, until slightly golden, about 2½ minutes. Season the tops of the chops with salt and pepper, turn them over, and cook for 2½ minutes longer. Transfer the pans to the oven and continue cooking until the chops are pink in the center when cut into with a knife, 5–6 minutes. Transfer the chops to a rack, tent loosely with aluminum foil, and let rest for 5 minutes. Gently reheat the sauce. Arrange the chops on warmed individual plates and spoon the warmed sauce on top. Scatter with parsley and serve.

MAKES 4 SERVINGS

DUXELLES SAUCE

The French term *duxelles* refers to diced fresh mushrooms, onions, and shallots sautéed in butter, a combination that is used in many French preparations. *Beurre manié* is simply a combination of butter and flour that is traditionally used to thicken a sauce without having clumps form. To make beurre manié for this recipe, mix together 1 tablespoon all-purpose (plain) flour and 1 tablespoon softened unsalted butter.

4 veal rib or loin chops, 8–10 oz (250–315 g) each

1½ tablespoons olive oil

Salt and freshly ground pepper

FOR THE SAUCE:

Beurre manié *(far left)*

3 tablespoons unsalted butter

½ yellow onion, very finely chopped

1 small shallot, very finely chopped

¼ lb (125 g) fresh white button or cremini mushrooms, brushed clean and very finely chopped

½ cup (4 fl oz/125 ml) dry white wine or vermouth

⅔ cup (5 fl oz/160 ml) canned beef consommé

⅓ cup (3 fl oz/80 ml) tomato purée

Salt and freshly ground pepper

Pinch of freshly grated nutmeg

Minced fresh flat-leaf (Italian) parsley for garnish

GRILLED PORK RIBS WITH BARBECUE SAUCE

FOR THE SAUCE:

2 tablespoons vegetable oil or bacon drippings

1 yellow onion, finely chopped

1 clove garlic, minced or pressed

1¾ cups (14 oz/440 g) ketchup

⅓ cup (3 fl oz/80 ml) Worcestershire sauce

½ teaspoon minced or grated lemon zest

3 tablespoons fresh lemon juice

2 tablespoons firmly packed dark brown sugar

1 teaspoon dry mustard

2½ teaspoons chile powder, preferably ancho

¼ teaspoon celery salt

Salt and freshly ground pepper

⅛ teaspoon Tabasco sauce, or to taste

5 lb (2.5 kg) pork loin back ribs

To make the sauce, in a large, heavy saucepan over medium heat, heat the vegetable oil. Add the onion and garlic and sauté until soft and translucent, about 5 minutes. Add the ketchup, Worcestershire sauce, lemon zest and juice, brown sugar, mustard, chile powder, celery salt, and a pinch of salt and stir to blend. Bring to a simmer, reduce the heat to low, and cook, uncovered, stirring occasionally, until slightly thickened, about 15 minutes. Transfer to a bowl and stir in the Tabasco. Season to taste with salt and pepper. Use the sauce at once, or let cool to room temperature, cover, and refrigerate for 1 day, to let the flavors meld, or for up to 2 weeks.

Preheat the oven to 325°F (165°C). Brush both sides of the ribs with a thin layer of the sauce and wrap tightly in heavy-duty aluminum foil. Place on a baking sheet and bake in the oven for 1¼ hours. Meanwhile, prepare a charcoal or gas grill for direct grilling over high heat. When the ribs are ready, remove the foil package from the oven and place it, seam side up, on the grill. Open the package, spreading the foil out to the sides, and poke about 20 holes in the foil around and underneath the ribs. Brush the ribs with sauce and grill for 15 minutes. Turn the ribs, brush the other side with sauce, and grill for 15 minutes longer. Check the meat for doneness; the bone should move freely in the sheath of meat, and the meat should be almost falling off the bone. If necessary, cook the ribs for 15–20 minutes longer, continuing to brush with sauce.

To serve, bring the remaining sauce to a boil and remove from the heat. Cut the meat into single-rib portions and pass the heated sauce at the table.

MAKES 6 SERVINGS

TABASCO SAUCE

Since 1870, the McIlhenny family of Louisiana has held the patent on the recipe for Tabasco sauce, the legendary hot sauce. The sauce is bottled on Avery Island, in the Gulf of Mexico, which has made it easier to keep the formula a secret. Few details of its production are known, except that Tabasco chiles are marinated in vinegar in wooden casks for three years before they are processed into sauce. In recent years, Tabasco's preeminence has been challenged by hundreds of new hot-pepper sauces made from a wide variety of chiles.

LAMB CURRY

CURRY POWDER

To make your own Madras curry powder, in a small frying pan over medium heat, toast 3 small dried New Mexico chiles or 1 ancho chile, 2 teaspoons *each* coriander seeds and cumin seeds, 1 teaspoon *each* peppercorns and fenugreek seeds, and ½ teaspoon mustard seeds until dark and aromatic, about 4 minutes. Grind to a powder in a mortar with a pestle or in a spice grinder, and mix with 1 tablespoon ground turmeric and ½ teaspoon ground ginger.

In a small bowl, whisk together the curry powder and ¼ cup (2 fl oz/60 ml) water (or more as needed) to form a paste; set the paste aside.

In a large frying pan over medium heat, heat 1 teaspoon of the oil. Add the almonds and sauté, shaking the pan constantly when they begin to sizzle, until golden brown, about 5 minutes. Using a slotted spoon, transfer the almonds to a bowl. Return the pan to medium heat and add 1 tablespoon of the oil. When it is hot, add the onion and sauté until soft and golden, about 6 minutes. Add the garlic and ¼ teaspoon salt and cook, stirring constantly, for 1 minute longer. Using a slotted spoon, transfer the onion mixture to a food processor and purée until smooth. Set aside.

Season the lamb generously with salt and pepper. In the frying pan over medium-high heat, heat the remaining 1 tablespoon oil. Working in batches if needed, brown the lamb on all sides, about 4 minutes. Reduce the heat to low, add the curry mixture, and cook, stirring to glaze the lamb, for 1 minute. Add the puréed onion mixture, tomatoes, soy sauce, honey, and a pinch of pepper.

Cover the pan and cook, simmering very gently, for 15 minutes. Check occasionally to be sure the paste is not too dry or it could scorch; if it seems dry, stir in 1–2 teaspoons water. Add the potatoes and coconut milk and cook, still covered, stirring occasionally, until the lamb and potatoes are tender, 30 minutes longer. Serve on warmed individual plates and garnish with the almonds.

Note: Prepared Madras curry powder is available in well-stocked markets and Asian grocery stores.

Serving Tip: Serve the lamb curry over basmati or jasmine rice.

MAKES 4 SERVINGS

¼ cup (¾ oz/20 g) Madras curry powder *(far left)*

1 teaspoon canola oil plus 2 tablespoons

⅓ cup (1½ oz/45 g) slivered blanched almonds

1 yellow onion, thinly sliced

3 cloves garlic, thinly sliced

Salt and freshly ground pepper

1¼ lb (625 g) leg of lamb or other lamb stewing meat, cut into 1-inch (2.5-cm) cubes

⅔ cup (5 oz/155 g) canned crushed tomatoes

2 tablespoons soy sauce

1 tablespoon honey

½ lb (250 g) boiling potatoes, peeled and cut into ½-inch (12-mm) cubes

1¼ cups (10 fl oz/310 ml) coconut milk

FILETS MIGNONS WITH BORDELAISE SAUCE

4 filets mignons, each
about 8 oz (250 g) and
2 inches (5 cm) thick

1½ tablespoons olive oil

FOR THE SAUCE:

1½ lb (750 g) beef
marrow bones, cut into
1½-inch (4-cm) lengths
by a butcher

2 teaspoons unsalted
butter

1 large shallot, minced

1¼ cups (10 fl oz/310 ml)
dry red wine such as
Cabernet Sauvignon

1 fresh thyme sprig

1 bay leaf

½ cup (4 fl oz/125 ml)
veal demi-glace (page 53)

Salt and freshly ground
pepper

1 tablespoon chilled
unsalted butter, cut into
2 pieces

Minced fresh flat-leaf
(Italian) parsley for garnish

Pat the filets dry with paper towels. Rub both sides of the filets with the olive oil and let stand at room temperature for 1 hour.

To make the sauce, put the marrow bones in a bowl filled with ice water and refrigerate for 20 minutes. Using your thumb, push the marrow out of the bones. If it won't budge, immerse the bones in warm water for about 30 seconds and try again. Cut the marrow into ½-inch (12-mm) disks, cover with fresh ice water, and refrigerate for 2–6 hours.

In a saucepan over low heat, melt the butter. Add the shallot and cook until translucent, about 5 minutes. Add the wine, thyme, and bay leaf, raise the heat to medium, and let simmer briskly until reduced by about three-fourths, 12–15 minutes. Remove and discard the herbs, and stir in the demi-glace and ¼ teaspoon *each* salt and pepper. Simmer, stirring occasionally, until slightly syrupy, 3–4 minutes. Turn off the heat, cover, and let stand.

Preheat the oven to 350°F (180°C). Set a large ovenproof frying pan over high heat. Season the filets generously on both sides with salt and pepper. When the pan is hot, add the filets and cook for about 2½ minutes. Turn them over and cook until firm and slightly brown, about 2½ minutes longer. Transfer the pan to the oven and cook 2–3 minutes longer for rare; 4–5 minutes for medium-rare. Turn off the oven, transfer the steaks to individual plates, and place them in the oven.

To finish the sauce, drain the marrow disks and add them to the sauce. Warm the sauce and marrow over low heat, about 3 minutes. Transfer a few pieces of marrow to top each filet. Remove the pan from the heat and whisk in the chilled butter until it melts and the sauce thickens slightly. Top each steak with several spoonfuls of the sauce, garnish with parsley, and serve.

MAKES 4 SERVINGS

BORDELAISE SAUCE

This famed sauce, which
is traditionally served with
panfried and grilled meats,
is a rich combination of red
wine, *sauce espagnole*
(brown sauce) or demi-glace,
and marrow, the soft, rich
tissue lodged in the hollow
center of beef bones. The
sauce originated in Bordeaux,
a well-known center of
gastronomy and arguably
France's most respected
wine region, with Mouton-
Rothschild, Château-Margaux,
and Château-Latour among
the local producers.

PORK SATAY WITH THAI PEANUT SAUCE

Soak 8 bamboo skewers in water for 30 minutes and drain, or use long metal skewers. In a large nonreactive bowl, combine the peanut oil, sesame oil, curry paste, 1 teaspoon salt, ¾ teaspoon black pepper, the garlic, and the red pepper flakes and whisk to blend. Add the pork and toss to coat evenly. Cover with plastic wrap and refrigerate for 6–8 hours.

To make the sauce, in a wok or frying pan over medium heat, heat the oil. Add the peanuts and fry, stirring constantly, until deep golden brown, about 3 minutes; do not let them burn. Using a slotted spoon, transfer to paper towels and let cool for 5 minutes. In a mini food processor, grind the peanuts finely and set aside.

Return the pan to low heat, add the garlic, shallots, and ¼ teaspoon salt and sauté for 1 minute. Add the fish sauce and sauté for 1 minute longer. Add the cayenne, brown sugar, soy sauce, and coconut milk and bring to a simmer. Stir in the peanuts and simmer, stirring occasionally, until the sauce is thickened, 6–7 minutes. Stir in the lemon juice. Taste and adjust the seasoning as desired.

Thread the pork cubes snugly onto the skewers and pat dry. If using bamboo skewers, wrap about 2 inches (5 cm) of the blunt end with aluminum foil for a handle. Preheat the broiler (grill). Line a rimmed baking sheet with aluminum foil, shiny side down, and top with a wire rack. Place in the broiler 4 inches (10 cm) from the heat source to preheat for 5 minutes.

Place the skewers on the rack, handles outward. Broil (grill), turning to sear all 4 sides, until well browned, about 2 minutes on each side. Divide the skewers evenly among 4 individual plates and remove the foil, if used, and sprinkle with the parsley. Put a small ramekin of the sauce on each plate and serve at once.

MAKES 4 SERVINGS

THAI INGREDIENTS
Thai fish sauce (nam pla) is slightly milder than the Vietnamese variety, but either may be used here. It may smell rather fishy, but when added to other ingredients, it mellows and supports the other flavors in the same way that salt does. Pungent Thai green curry paste contains green bird's-eye chiles, galangal (a close relative of ginger), lemongrass, kaffir lime, shallot, garlic, and shrimp (prawn) paste. Once opened, it will keep in the refrigerator for up to 2 months. Always shake canned coconut milk before using, as the fat rises to the top.

¼ cup (2 fl oz/60 ml) peanut oil

1 tablespoon sesame oil

1 tablespoon Thai green curry paste

Salt and ground pepper

1 large clove garlic, minced

Pinch of red pepper flakes

1¼ lb (625 g) boneless pork loin, cubed

FOR THE SAUCE:

2 tablespoons peanut oil

¾ cup (4½ oz/140 g) raw or roasted peanut halves

1 large clove garlic, minced

2 shallots, minced

Salt

4 teaspoons Asian fish sauce

¼ teaspoon cayenne pepper

½ teaspoon brown sugar

1½ teaspoons soy sauce

1¼ cups (10 fl oz/310 ml) coconut milk

1 tablespoon lemon juice

Sprigs of fresh flat-leaf (Italian) parsley for garnish

CHICKEN WITH MOLE SAUCE

Tear or cut open the mulato, ancho, and pasilla chiles lengthwise, and remove the seeds and veins. Tear or cut the chiles into ½-inch (12-mm) pieces.

In a heavy frying pan over medium heat, melt 2 tablespoons of the lard. Add the chiles and sauté, tossing frequently, until slightly charred but not burned, about 2 minutes. Using a slotted spoon, transfer the chiles to a bowl and add warm water to cover. Let stand for 2–4 hours.

Meanwhile, in a large bowl, combine the fire-roasted tomatoes and chocolate. With a mortar and pestle or in a spice grinder, grind the peppercorns, clove, allspice berries, and cinnamon. Stir the spices into the tomato mixture and set aside.

In a heavy dry frying pan over medium heat, toast all the sesame seeds, shaking the pan once or twice, until deep golden, about 30 seconds. Reserving some for garnish, add 2 tablespoons of the sesame seeds to the tomato mixture. Repeat the process with the coriander seeds and add all of them to the tomato mixture.

Wipe out the frying pan used to toast the chiles with a paper towel, place over medium heat, and melt 2 tablespoons of the lard. Add the almonds and toast, stirring occasionally, until nicely browned, about 4 minutes. Using a slotted spoon, add them to the tomato mixture. Repeat with the raisins. Repeat with the onion and garlic, cooking each until golden brown, about 5 minutes. Press down on the ingredients with the back of the spoon to remove excess fat before transferring them to the bowl. Add more lard to the pan if necessary, brown the bread on all sides, about 2 minutes, and stir into the tomato mixture.

Transfer half of the tomato mixture to a blender, add ½ cup (4 fl oz/ 125 ml) of the stock, and purée until smooth. Pass the mixture through the coarse shredding disk of a food mill into a bowl.

Ingredients

3 mulato chiles (if unavailable, use 3 additional ancho chiles)

2 ancho chiles

4 pasilla chiles

6 tablespoons (3 oz/90 g) lard or 6 tablespoons (3 fl oz/90 ml) vegetable oil, or as needed

½ cup (3 oz/90 g) canned crushed fire-roasted tomatoes

1 oz (30 g) Mexican chocolate *(far right)*, chopped

10 peppercorns

1 whole clove

2 whole allspice berries or ⅛ teaspoon ground allspice

1½-inch (4-cm) piece cinnamon stick, broken into pieces

2 tablespoons sesame seeds, plus more for garnish

¼ teaspoon coriander seeds

2 tablespoons almonds

2 tablespoons raisins

½ small yellow onion, thickly sliced

WORKING WITH CHILES

When working with fresh or (as in this recipe) dried hot chiles, you may wish to wear thin disposable gloves, as the chiles' volatile oils can cause irritation if they come into contact with your skin. Whether or not you wear gloves, avoid touching your eyes, nose, or mouth while working with chiles. Contact lens wearers should be particularly cautious: Once a lens is contaminated by rubbing or touching your eye, it must be discarded, because the oil cannot be soaked or washed off.

24

2 small cloves garlic

2 thick slices day-old French bread, crusts removed, torn into 1-inch (2.5-cm) pieces

3½–4 cups (28–32 fl oz/ 875 ml–1 l) chicken stock (page 112)

1 chicken, about 3½ lb (1.75 kg), cut into serving pieces

Salt and freshly ground pepper

2 tablespoons sugar

Cooked tortillas, warmed, for serving (optional)

Repeat with the remaining tomato mixture and ½ cup of the stock and add to the bowl. Set aside.

Drain the soaked chiles, squeezing them gently; reserve ½ cup (4 fl oz/125 ml) of the soaking water. Transfer the chiles and water to the blender (there is no need to wash the blender) and blend until smooth. Pass the purée through the food mill (again, no need to wash) into a separate bowl.

Season the chicken with salt and pepper. In a large, heavy casserole or Dutch oven over medium-high heat, heat the remaining 2 tablespoons lard. Working in batches, add the chicken and cook until golden, about 4 minutes on each side. Transfer to a platter.

Pour off all but about 1 tablespoon of the fat from the pot and set over low heat. Add the puréed chiles and cook, scraping the bottom of the pan occasionally, for about 5 minutes; the mixture should be quite dark and thick. Add the tomato mixture and cook, stirring occasionally, until the sauce thickens and is evenly blended, about 4 minutes. Stir in the remaining 2½ cups (20 fl oz/ 625 ml) stock, cover partially, and let simmer gently, stirring occasionally, for 45 minutes. Add 1½ teaspoons salt and the sugar. If the sauce is thicker than heavy (double) cream, thin with a little more stock.

Preheat the oven to 350°F (180°C). Return the chicken to the pot, spoon over the sauce, and cover. Transfer to the oven and cook until tender, with no trace of pink at the bone, about 1 hour. Remove from the oven and spoon off any fat from the surface. Garnish with reserved toasted sesame seeds and serve with warmed tortillas, if desired.

MAKES 4 SERVINGS

(Photograph appears on following page.)

MEXICAN CHOCOLATE

The chocolate in mole contributes a deep richness without making the sauce sweet. So-called Mexican chocolate, often used for making hot chocolate, has a grainier texture than common baking or eating chocolate and contains cinnamon and sometimes almonds. If Mexican chocolate is not available, substitute 1 ounce (30 g) dark, semisweet (plain) chocolate, ½ teaspoon ground cinnamon, and a drop of almond extract (essence).

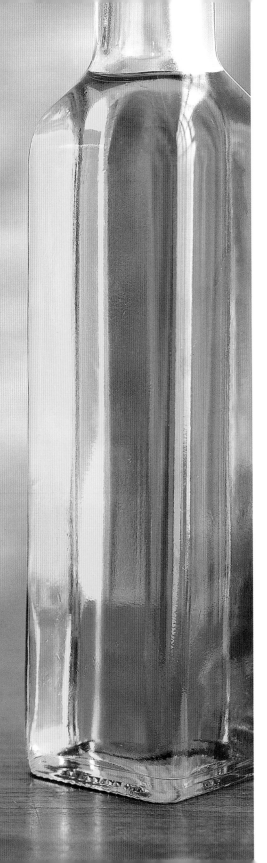

VINAIGRETTES AND EMULSIONS

Some of the world's great sauces are emulsions, including garlic-spiked aioli and the versatile family of vinaigrettes. In this chapter, a warm bacon vinaigrette adds zip to escarole, while smooth-as-silk beurre blanc lends sophistication to sautéed sea bass and a bright sabayon sauce livens up roast leg of lamb.

MÂCHE AND BEET SALAD
WITH SHERRY VINAIGRETTE

To make the vinaigrette, in a small bowl, whisk together the shallot, mustard, vinegar, ½ teaspoon salt, and ¼ teaspoon pepper. Slowly pour in the oil in a fine, steady stream, whisking constantly until a smooth, thick emulsion forms, about 1 minute. Refrigerate to let the flavors meld; just before tossing the vinaigrette with the mâche, whisk again and stir in the herbs, if using.

Preheat the oven to 375°F (190°C). Put the beets in the center of a large piece of aluminum foil and top each with a thyme sprig. Drizzle each beet with ¼ teaspoon of the olive oil and season with a pinch each of salt and pepper. Bring up the sides of the packet and seal securely. Place on a baking sheet and bake until the beets are tender when pierced with a sharp knife, 45–60 minutes. Remove from the oven and let cool in the foil, then unwrap. Remove the skins with your fingers or a pairing knife.

In a small, nonstick frying pan over medium-low heat, heat the remaining ¼ teaspoon olive oil. Add the pecans and toast, tossing occasionally, until fragrant and slightly golden, 1–2 minutes. Season with a pinch of salt and transfer the pecans to a plate.

Using a mandoline or a sharp knife, cut the beets into very thin slices. Divide among chilled individual plates or arrange on a serving platter, fanning out the beets decoratively. In a bowl, toss the mâche with just enough of the vinaigrette to coat the leaves. Place a mound of mâche on top of each serving of beets. Scatter the pecans over the salads and serve.

Note: Also called field salad, corn salad, or lamb's lettuce (because it appears in early spring), mâche is a mild, delicate salad green with oval leaves that grow in small, loose bunches.

MAKES 4 SERVINGS

VINAIGRETTE VARIATIONS

The most basic vinaigrette contains only oil, vinegar, salt, and pepper. Olive oil and sherry vinegar are used in this recipe, but dozens of variations are possible. Try substituting lemon or orange juice for some of the vinegar, and add a teaspoon of citrus zest to enhance the flavor. Other great vinaigrette ingredients include snipped fresh chives and finely chopped shallots. Add these to the mixture just before the oil.

FOR THE VINAIGRETTE:

½ small shallot, minced

2 teaspoons Dijon mustard

2 tablespoons sherry vinegar

Salt and freshly ground pepper

7 tablespoons (3½ fl oz/ 105 ml) extra-virgin olive oil

2 teaspoons minced fresh herbs such as tarragon, chives, basil, or chervil (optional)

4 small beets, about 3 oz (90 g) each

4 small fresh thyme sprigs

1¼ teaspoons extra-virgin olive oil

Salt and freshly ground pepper

½ cup (2 oz/60 g) pecan halves

4 cups (4 oz/125 g) loosely packed mâche (see Note)

ESCAROLE SALAD WITH WARM BACON VINAIGRETTE

¼ lb (125 g) thick-cut bacon, cut into ½-inch (12-mm) pieces

1 large head escarole (Batavian endive), tough, dark-green outer leaves discarded

1 tablespoon olive oil

1 clove garlic, lightly crushed

1 tablespoon sherry vinegar

2 teaspoons sherry wine

2 tablespoons walnut or pistachio oil *(far right)*

Salt and freshly ground pepper

⅓ cup (1½ oz/45 g) coarsely chopped walnuts or pistachios

Bring a small saucepan three-fourths full of water to a boil over high heat. Add the bacon and cook until pale and puffy, about 5 minutes. Drain, then transfer to paper towels to dry.

Tear the escarole leaves into bite-sized pieces. Wash and dry them and put in a wide salad bowl.

In a frying pan over medium heat, heat the olive oil. Add the garlic and bacon and cook, stirring occasionally, until the garlic is golden (do not let it burn) and the bacon is crisp and browned, 3–5 minutes. Remove the garlic and discard. Add the vinegar and sherry wine and bring to a boil, then pour the mixture over the escarole. Using tongs, immediately toss to coat the leaves evenly and wilt them slightly. Drizzle the walnut oil over the salad, add ½ teaspoon salt and ¼ teaspoon pepper, and toss again. Scatter the walnuts over the salad and serve at once.

MAKES 4 SERVINGS

NUT OILS

Using nut oils, such as walnut, hazelnut (filbert), or pistachio, is a wonderful way to vary the flavor of a vinaigrette. Substitute a nut oil for only half—not all—of the oil called for in a vinaigrette; otherwise the flavor can be overwhelming. A little pistachio oil is perfect with grilled-chicken salad or steamed asparagus; delicate hazelnut oil complements a trout salad or a mélange of wild mushrooms; and walnut oil is superb on any of the relatives of escarole: Belgian endive (witloof/chicory), frisée, and radicchio.

SEARED TUNA WITH ITALIAN SALSA VERDE

To make the salsa, in a mini food processor, combine the anchovies, garlic, parsley, mint, capers, mustard, and vinegar. (If using regular anchovies, soak first in warm water to cover for 5 minutes, drain, and pat dry.) Purée until smooth. With the motor running, drizzle in the olive oil in a steady stream and process until smooth. Cover and refrigerate for at least 1 hour to let the flavors meld.

Season both sides of the tuna steaks generously with salt and pepper and let stand for 5 minutes. Heat a large cast-iron pan or stove-top griddle over high heat. Add the canola oil. When the oil is hot, add the tuna and sear for 1½ minutes. Turn the tuna over and sear until the tuna just begins to brown, about 1½ minutes longer. If you like the center quite rare, serve at once. Or, reduce the heat to low and cook for 1 minute longer on each side for medium, or 3–4 minutes longer for well done.

Transfer the tuna to warmed individual plates and top each piece with a large spoonful of salsa verde. Serve at once.

MAKES 4 SERVINGS

SALSA VERDE

The Mexican version of *salsa verde*, based on tomatillos, is perhaps better known, but this salty, piquant Italian sauce also has a devoted following. Spanish white anchovies, sometimes labeled *boquerones en vinagre*, are preferred in this recipe because of their mildness. Look for salt-packed capers, which have a better flavor than those packed in brine. If using salt-packed capers, rinse them before using. Finally, do not substitute curly parsley for the flat-leaf parsley; the flavor of the sauce will be lacking.

FOR THE SALSA:

2 Spanish white anchovy fillets *(far left)* or 1 regular oil-packed anchovy fillet

1 clove garlic, minced

1¼ cups (2½ oz/75 g) firmly packed fresh flat-leaf (Italian) parsley leaves

¼ cup (½ oz/15 g) firmly packed fresh mint leaves

1 tablespoon capers, rinsed

1 teaspoon Dijon mustard

1½ teaspoons white or red wine vinegar

⅓ cup (3 fl oz/80 ml) extra-virgin olive oil

4 sushi-grade ahi tuna steaks, each 5–6 oz (155–185 g) and about 1¼ inches (3 cm) thick

Salt and freshly ground pepper

1 teaspoon canola oil

DEEP-FRIED ZUCCHINI WITH AIOLI

FOR THE AIOLI:

2 or 3 large cloves garlic, sliced

Salt and freshly ground white pepper

1 whole large egg plus 1 large egg yolk, at room temperature

1 teaspoon white wine vinegar

1 teaspoon Dijon mustard

½ cup (4 fl oz/125 ml) extra-virgin olive oil

¾ cup (6 fl oz/180 ml) canola oil

1 tablespoon boiling water

1 tablespoon fresh lemon juice

1 lb (500 g) small green and yellow zucchini (courgettes)

½ cup (2 oz/60 g) rice flour

1 teaspoon paprika

Salt and freshly ground white pepper

⅛ teaspoon cayenne pepper

Canola oil for deep-frying

To make the aioli, in a mortar with a pestle, pound together the garlic and ½ teaspoon salt until a smooth paste forms. Scrape the mixture into a mini food processor and add the egg, egg yolk, vinegar, and mustard. Process until blended. With the motor running, slowly drizzle in the olive and canola oils; you can begin to add them more quickly once the mixture emulsifies. Add the boiling water, lemon juice, and ¼ teaspoon white pepper and pulse 2 or 3 times. Cover and refrigerate until serving.

Trim the ends off the zucchini, cut crosswise into 2½-inch (6.5-cm) lengths, and then quarter each piece lengthwise. In a large bowl, stir together the rice flour, paprika, ¾ teaspoon salt, ¼ teaspoon white pepper, and cayenne. Add the zucchini pieces, toss to coat evenly, then transfer to a colander and shake gently to remove excess flour.

Preheat the oven to 150°F (65°C). Pour canola oil to a depth of 2 inches (5 cm) into a heavy, deep frying pan or wide saucepan and heat to 375°F (190°C) on a deep-frying thermometer. Working in batches, add the vegetables to the hot oil and deep-fry until golden brown, about 5 minutes. Using a wire skimmer or slotted spoon, transfer to paper towels to drain briefly, then place on a heatproof plate in the oven. Reheat until all the zucchini are fried.

To serve, place a bowl of the aioli on a platter; surround with the fried zucchini, and sprinke the zucchini with salt.

Note: This recipe contains uncooked eggs. For more information, see page 115.

MAKES 4–6 SERVINGS

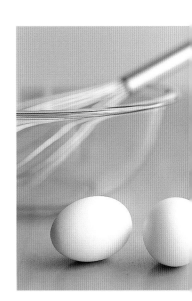

MAYONNAISE VARIATIONS

Aioli is one variation on mayonnaise, a classic emulsion sauce. Rémoulade is yet another variation. To make rémoulade, proceed as for the aioli, but use only 1 clove garlic and stir 2 tablespoons Dijon mustard, ¼ cup (2 oz/ 60 g) finely chopped capers, 1 tablespoon *each* minced fresh flat-leaf (Italian) parsley and tarragon, and 1 teaspoon anchovy paste into the finished mayonnaise. Serve with blanched green beans or celery root (celeriac).

SAUTÉED SEA BASS WITH BEURRE BLANC

To make the beurre blanc, in a small saucepan over medium-high heat, combine the wine, vinegar, and shallot and bring to a boil. Reduce the heat to low and simmer gently until reduced to about 1 tablespoon, about 12 minutes. Watch carefully so the liquid does not completely evaporate. Remove from the heat.

While the wine mixture is reducing, begin cooking the fish: Pat the sea bass fillets dry with paper towels and season both sides with salt and white pepper. In a large, nonstick frying pan over medium heat, melt the 1 tablespoon butter. When the foam begins to subside and the butter is just beginning to brown, swirl the pan to coat it evenly. Add the fillets and cook until just beginning to brown, about 2 minutes. Carefully turn the fillets over and cook until firm to the touch and just opaque through to the center when tested with a knife, about 2 minutes longer.

To finish the sauce, return the wine mixture to low heat. Add the ⅓ cup butter all at once and whisk constantly until the butter melts and is emulsified. Add ¼ teaspoon *each* salt and white pepper and the 2 tablespoons chives and whisk again. Remove from the heat, cover, and serve the sauce within 5 minutes.

To serve, transfer the fillets to warmed individual plates, top with the beurre blanc, and scatter with the chives.

MAKES 4 SERVINGS

BEURRE BLANC

Beurre blanc ("white butter") is a simple yet elegant sauce in which the main emulsifier is butter instead of eggs. Some say the sauce was "discovered" by accident when a chef in southern France forgot the eggs when making a béarnaise and was surprised by the successful result. Beurre blanc is traditionally made with a crisp white wine such as Sauvignon Blanc or Sancerre, and because it is rather delicate, the sauce goes well with tender white fish such as sea bass.

⅔ cup (5 fl oz/160 ml) dry white wine such as Sauvignon Blanc

2 tablespoons white wine vinegar or Champagne vinegar

1 large shallot, minced

4 sea bass fillets or other white fish fillets, each 6–7 oz (185–220 g) and about ½ inch (12 mm) thick

Salt and freshly ground white pepper

1 tablespoon plus ⅓ cup (3 oz/90 g) unsalted butter, at room temperature, cut into 6 pieces

2 tablespoons finely snipped fresh chives (page 114), plus more for garnish

ROAST LEG OF LAMB WITH RED PEPPER SABAYON

3 tablespoons minced
garlic (4–6 cloves)

Salt and freshly ground
black pepper

2 tablespoons olive oil

1 bone-in leg of lamb,
4–5 lb (2–2.5 kg)

1 whole lemon, peel on,
thinly sliced

FOR THE SABAYON:

1 red bell pepper
(capsicum)

¼ cup (4 fl oz/125 ml) dry
white wine or vermouth

4 large egg yolks

4 tablespoons (2 oz/60 g)
unsalted butter, chilled
and cut into 8 pieces

Salt and freshly ground
white pepper

2 teaspoons minced
fresh mint

Preheat the oven to 500°F (260°C). In a bowl, combine the garlic, 1 tablespoon salt, 1½ teaspoons black pepper, and the olive oil and mix well. Using a small, sharp knife, cut 10 slits, each about 1½ inches (4 cm) deep, into the lamb. Push some of the garlic mixture into the slits and rub the rest over the outside of the lamb.

Line a roasting pan with aluminum foil, shiny side down, and arrange the lemon slices on the foil in a single layer. Put the lamb on top and roast for 20 minutes. Reduce the oven temperature to 300°F (150°C) and roast until an instant-read thermometer inserted into the thickest part of the lamb away from the bone registers 130°F (54°C), 30–40 minutes longer. Transfer the lamb to a carving board, tent with aluminum foil, and let rest for 10–15 minutes.

Roast the bell pepper *(right)* and cut into 1-inch (2.5-cm) pieces. Transfer to a food processor, add the wine, and purée until smooth. Cool the purée to room temperature. Place the egg yolks in a stainless-steel bowl and whisk in the pepper purée. Set the bowl over (but not touching) barely simmering water in a saucepan. Whisk until the mixture is thickened and doubled in volume and you can begin to see the base of the bowl as you whisk, about 7 minutes. Whisk in the butter 2 pieces at a time until smooth. Remove from the heat and stir in ½ teaspoon salt and ¼ teaspoon white pepper. Fold in the mint. Serve at once.

Carve the lamb into thin slices and serve on warmed individual plates. Transfer the sabayon to a sauceboat and pass alongside.

Variation Tip: To make Lemon Sabayon, omit the bell pepper in the sabayon recipe, above, and substitute 1 tablespoon fresh lemon juice.

Note: This dish contains eggs that may be only partially cooked. For more information, see page 115.

MAKES 6 SERVINGS

ROASTING PEPPERS

You can roast peppers by holding them directly over a gas flame on a stove top or placing them in a broiler (grill). In either case, turn with tongs until the skin is blistered and blackened on all sides; be careful not to let the flesh burn. Put the blackened peppers into a paper bag, close tightly, and let stand for 10 minutes, then peel off the charred skin with your fingers. Slit the peppers lengthwise; remove the stems, seeds, and membranes; and cut as desired.

41

STEAMED SALMON WITH CHARMOULA

To make the *charmoula*, with the motor of a food processor running, add the garlic cloves one at a time until finely minced. Then add the cilantro, parsley, lemon juice, 1 teaspoon salt, the paprika, cumin, and cayenne to taste and purée until smooth. Slowly add the oil, processing until smooth and emulsified. Measure 3 tablespoons of the sauce and reserve. Put the remaining sauce in a serving bowl, cover, and refrigerate.

Put the salmon on a platter and rub both sides of the fish with the 3 tablespoons sauce. Cover with plastic wrap and refrigerate for at least 2 hours.

Remove the fish and the remaining sauce from the refrigerator and let stand at room temperature for 20 minutes.

Pour water to a depth of 1 inch (2.5 cm) in a large steamer pan or other large pot and bring to a simmer over medium-low heat. Set a steamer rack or other large, round rack over the simmering water. Arrange the salmon fillets on a heatproof plate, place the plate on the rack, cover the pan tightly, and steam until the fish is firm to the touch and is barely opaque throughout when tested with a knife, about 8 minutes.

Transfer the fish to warmed individual plates and top each fillet with a generous spoonful of the *charmoula*. Pass the remaining sauce at the table.

MAKES 4 SERVINGS

CHARMOULA

Charmoula is a classic Moroccan preparation that can be used as a marinade or a sauce and is commonly served with fish. It features many familiar Mediterranean ingredients, but extra doses of paprika and cumin give it a distinctly North African character. To make the sauce without a food processor, mince the garlic or push it through a press, chop the cilantro and parsley leaves very finely, and combine with the garlic and herbs in nonreactive bowl. Add the remaining ingredients and whisk until smooth.

FOR THE CHARMOULA:

4 cloves garlic

⅓ cup (⅔ oz/20 g) firmly packed fresh cilantro (fresh coriander) leaves

⅓ cup (⅔ oz/20 g) firmly packed fresh flat-leaf (Italian) parsley leaves

¼ cup (2 fl oz/60 ml) fresh lemon juice

Salt

1½ teaspoons paprika

¾ teaspoon ground cumin

⅛–¼ teaspoon cayenne pepper

½ cup (4 fl oz/125 ml) extra-virgin olive oil

4 center-cut salmon fillets, about 6 oz (185 g) each, skin removed

PAN SAUCES

When you take advantage of the caramelized glaze that forms in a pan in which you have sautéed or roasted meat, poultry, or fish, the result is a sauce that is rich, flavorful, and easy to make. A French classic, brown butter sauce is a simple finish to a sautéed skate wing, and a piquant three-peppercorn sauce is a quick-to-assemble accompaniment to pork medallions.

SAUTÉED CHICKEN BREASTS
WITH WHOLE-GRAIN MUSTARD SAUCE
46

ROAST CHICKEN WITH PAN GRAVY
49

ENTRECÔTE OF BEEF
WITH MARCHAND DE VIN SAUCE
50

SAUTÉED LAMB CHOPS WITH BALSAMIC REDUCTION
53

SEARED PORK MEDALLIONS
WITH THREE-PEPPERCORN SAUCE
54

SKATE WINGS WITH
BROWN BUTTER AND CAPER SAUCE
57

PORK CHOPS WITH
PORT AND DRIED CHERRY SAUCE
58

SAUTÉED CHICKEN BREASTS
WITH WHOLE-GRAIN MUSTARD SAUCE

Place a large baking dish in the oven and preheat to 150°F (65°C).

Rinse the chicken breasts and pat them dry with paper towels. Using a meat pounder, lightly pound the breasts to an even thickness of just under ½ inch (12 mm). Season both sides with salt and pepper.

In a large frying pan over medium-high heat, melt the butter with the oil. When the foam begins to subside, add the chicken breasts without crowding and cook, without moving them, until just beginning to brown, about 2 minutes. Turn the chicken over and cook until firm to the touch and there is no sign of pink in the center when tested with a knife, 2–2½ minutes longer. Transfer the chicken breasts to the baking dish in the oven.

To make the mustard sauce, return the frying pan to medium-low heat and add the shallot. Cook, stirring, until slightly softened, about 1 minute. Add the wine and raise the heat to medium-high. Simmer, stirring with a wooden spoon to scrape up the flavorful bits from the bottom and sides of the pan, until the wine is reduced to about 2 tablespoons, 2–3 minutes. Stir in the cream, ½ teaspoon salt, and ¼ teaspoon pepper and bring to a boil. Simmer, stirring frequently, until the sauce is thick enough to coat the back of the spoon, 1–2 minutes. Remove from the heat and immediately whisk in the mustard just until smooth.

Transfer the chicken breasts to warmed individual plates. Top each with 2 or 3 spoonfuls of the sauce and serve at once.

MAKES 4 SERVINGS

DEGLAZING

When meat, fish, or poultry is sautéed in a pan with butter or oil, the caramelizing process results in a "fond," a coating of browned, flavorful bits on the bottom of the pan. In order to incorporate this tasty residue into the sauce, once the meat has been removed, the pan is deglazed by adding a liquid, often wine or stock, and stirring and scraping. The liquid softens the fond, enabling it to be loosened with a wooden spoon and mixed into the final sauce.

4 skinless, boneless chicken breast halves

Salt and freshly ground pepper

2 teaspoons unsalted butter

2 teaspoons canola or olive oil

FOR THE MUSTARD SAUCE:

1 shallot, minced

½ cup (4 fl oz/125 ml) dry white wine or vermouth

¾ cup (6 fl oz/180 ml) heavy (double) cream

Salt and freshly ground pepper

3 tablespoons whole-grain mustard

ROAST CHICKEN WITH PAN GRAVY

1 chicken, 3½–4 lb
(1.75–2 kg)

Salt and freshly ground
pepper

6 unpeeled garlic cloves,
crushed

4 fresh thyme sprigs

4 fresh rosemary sprigs

2 tablespoons unsalted
butter, melted

1 cup (8 fl oz/250 ml) dry
white wine or vermouth

FOR THE PAN GRAVY:

2 tablespoons all-purpose
(plain) flour

2 tablespoons sherry
(optional)

1 cup (8 fl oz/250 ml)
chicken stock (page 112)
or prepared broth

¼ cup (2 fl oz/60 ml)
heavy (double) cream

Salt and freshly ground
pepper

1–2 tablespoons Dijon
mustard, or to taste
(optional)

Preheat the oven to 400°F (200°C). Rinse the chicken inside and out and pat dry with paper towels. Season generously inside and out with salt and pepper. Put the garlic, thyme, and rosemary inside the cavity. Place the chicken, breast side up, on a rack in a roasting pan (there is no need to truss it). Brush the chicken with the melted butter.

Place the pan in the oven with the chicken's legs toward the rear. Roast until the skin begins to brown, about 40 minutes. Reduce the oven temperature to 325°F (165°C) and pour the wine into the pan. Roast, turning the chicken on its breast for part of the time, until an instant-read thermometer inserted into the thickest part of the thigh (away from the bone) registers 170°F (77°C), or until the juices run clear when a thigh is pierced with a knife, about 40–45 minutes longer. Turn off the oven, transfer the chicken to an ovenproof platter, and place it in the oven with the door ajar.

To make the gravy, pour the pan juices into a glass measuring pitcher and let stand for 1 minute. Take 1–2 tablespoons of the fat from the surface and return it to the pan. Set the pan on the stove top over medium heat, add the flour, and cook, stirring, for about 2 minutes, watching closely so that it does not burn. Drizzle in the sherry, if using, and stock and cook, stirring to scrape up the flavorful bits from the bottom and sides of the pan, about 2 minutes. Skim off the remaining fat from the pan juices and discard. Return the juices to the pan, bring to a simmer, and cook for 2 minutes. Whisk in the cream and simmer until slightly thickened, about 1 minute longer. Season to taste with salt and pepper. Whisk in the mustard, if using.

Carve the chicken and serve. Pour the gravy into a sauceboat and pass at the table.

MAKES 4 SERVINGS

ROASTING TIPS

A roast chicken is one of the easiest dishes to make, and yet also one of the trickiest to get absolutely right. Three simple tips will help guarantee success. First, make sure the chicken is at room temperature to ensure even cooking. Second, dry the chicken well after rinsing it. If there is too much moisture, the chicken will steam rather than roast. Finally, always put the chicken into the oven with the legs toward the rear, hotter part of the oven. The breast cooks more quickly than the legs, and thus is less likely to overcook if it is toward the front.

ENTRECÔTE OF BEEF
WITH MARCHAND DE VIN SAUCE

To make *marchand de vin* butter, in a saucepan, combine the wine and shallot. Simmer over low heat until reduced to about 2 tablespoons, 12–15 minutes. Let cool. Meanwhile, in a bowl, combine the butter, lemon juice, and parsley. Whisk in the cooled wine mixture, ¼ teaspoon salt, and a pinch of pepper. Set aside.

Place a large baking dish in the oven and preheat to 150°F (65°C). Pat the steaks dry with paper towels and season both sides generously with salt and pepper.

In a large nonreactive frying pan over high heat, heat the oil. Just before it begins to smoke, add the steaks and cook, without moving them, for 2½ minutes. Turn the steaks over and cook for 2 minutes longer for rare, 3 minutes longer for medium-rare, or 4 minutes longer for medium-well. Transfer the steaks to the baking dish in the oven.

Immediately pour off the fat from the frying pan and pour in the wine and water. Set the pan over high heat and cook, stirring to scrape up the flavorful bits from the bottom and sides of the pan, until the liquid is reduced to about 1 tablespoon. Remove from the heat and let cool slightly, about 1½ minutes. Add ½ cup (4 oz/125 g) of *marchand de vin* butter (you will have some left over) and whisk until the sauce emulsifies and thickens slightly.

Transfer the steaks to warmed individual plates. Top each steak with several spoonfuls of the sauce and serve at once.

Note: Entrecôte, similar to rib-eye, is a particularly tender boneless cut of beef from the rib section.

MAKES 2 SERVINGS

FOR THE MARCHAND DE VIN BUTTER:

1 cup (8 fl oz/250 ml) dry red wine

1 shallot, minced

¾ cup (6 oz/185 g) unsalted butter, diced, at room temperature

1 tablespoon fresh lemon juice

1 tablespoon minced flat-leaf (Italian) parsley

Salt and freshly ground pepper

2 entrecôte (see Note), rib-eye, or New York steaks, 8 oz (250 g) each

Salt and freshly ground pepper

2 teaspoons canola or olive oil

½ cup (4 fl oz/125 ml) dry red wine

2 tablespoons water

SAUTÉED LAMB CHOPS WITH BALSAMIC REDUCTION

8–12 lamb loin chops, each about 1½ inches (4 cm) thick

Salt and freshly ground pepper

2 teaspoons canola oil

2 teaspoons unsalted butter

1 oz (30 g) prosciutto, finely chopped

1 large leek, white part only, finely chopped, or 2 shallots, minced

½ cup (4 fl oz/125 ml) good-quality balsamic vinegar

½ cup (4 fl oz/125 ml) veal demi-glace *(far right)* or 1 cup (8 fl oz/250 ml) beef stock, reduced to ½ cup

Let the lamb chops come to room temperature for 30 minutes. Pat them dry with paper towels and season both sides generously with salt and pepper.

Place a large baking dish in the oven and preheat to 150°F (65°C). In a large frying pan over medium-high heat, heat the oil. When it just begins to smoke, add the chops and cook, without moving them, for 2½–3 minutes. Turn the chops over and continue cooking for 2½–3 minutes longer. Using tongs, sear the fat-lined edge of each chop for about 15 seconds. Transfer the chops to the baking dish in the oven.

Wipe out the pan with a paper towel and return it to medium heat. Melt the butter, add the prosciutto and leek, and cook, stirring, until the leek is soft and the prosciutto is golden, about 2 minutes. Raise the heat to medium-high and add the balsamic vinegar. Simmer, stirring to scrape up all the flavorful bits from the bottom and sides of the pan, until the liquid is reduced by two-thirds, about 1½ minutes. Stir in the demi-glace, ¼ teaspoon salt, and a pinch of pepper. Bring to a simmer and cook for 1 minute longer.

Transfer the chops to warmed individual plates and serve with several spoonfuls of the sauce.

Note: Lamb loin chops are small in size; allow 2 per person for light eaters, 3 for heartier eaters.

MAKES 4–6 SERVINGS

DEMI-GLACE

Veal demi-glace, a building block of many classic sauces, is a mixture of stock, brown sauce, and wine that has been reduced to yield an intense depth of flavor. In the past, cooks had to make it at home—a time-consuming task—but now it is available in better supermarkets and gourmet stores. Commercial veal demi-glace varies in consistency; if your final sauce is too thick, add a teaspoon or two of water. If necessary, you can substitute homemade beef stock that has been reduced by half, but the resulting sauce will be far less distinctive.

SEARED PORK MEDALLIONS
WITH THREE-PEPPERCORN SAUCE

Place a baking dish in the oven and preheat to 150°F (65°C). Pat the pork medallions dry with paper towels. Using a meat pounder, lightly pound them to an even thickness of about 1¼ inches (3 cm). Rub with the oil and let stand for 15 minutes. On a plate, combine the black and white peppercorns. Push the medallions into the peppercorns, pressing firmly so they adhere.

Set a large frying pan over medium-high heat. Sprinkle both sides of each medallion with a tiny pinch of salt. When the pan is very hot, place the medallions, salted side down, in the pan (do not crowd). Cook, without moving or pressing down on them, until lightly browned on the bottom, about 2½ minutes. Season the tops of each medallion with a tiny pinch of salt, turn them over, and cook, without moving them, for 1 minute. Reduce the heat to very low and cook until just firm to the touch, about 1½ minutes longer. Transfer to the baking dish in the oven.

Wipe out the pan and return it to medium heat. Melt the butter, add the shallot, and sauté until slightly soft, about 2 minutes. Add the green peppercorns and cook, stirring, for 1 minute. Return the medallions and any accumulated juices to the pan, add the Cognac and ½ teaspoon salt, and raise the heat to medium-high. Shake the pan gently for 1 minute, then add the cream and demi-glace. Swirl to combine and simmer for 1 minute longer, then spoon the sauce over the pork. Season to taste with salt. Transfer the medallions to warmed individual plates and top with several spoonfuls of the sauce. Serve at once.

Note: Pork medallions are small, boneless cuts from the tenderloin.

MAKES 4 SERVINGS

PEPPERCORNS

Black, white, and green peppercorns all come from the same plant, *Piper nigrum*. Black peppercorns are the unripe berries of the plant; they are fermented and sun-dried, which turns their skins dark. White peppercorns are ripe, as they remain on the plant longer. Once harvested, they are soaked and their skin removed to reveal white seeds. They are milder than black peppercorns. Fresh-tasting green peppercorns are picked unripe and then preserved by drying or bottling in brine.

8 pork medallions, 3 oz (90 g) each, trimmed of excess fat (see Note)

1 tablespoon canola or olive oil

1 tablespoon coarsely cracked black peppercorns

1½ teaspoons coarsely cracked white peppercorns

Salt

1 tablespoon unsalted butter

1 large shallot, minced

2 tablespoons green peppercorns, drained if packed in brine (far left)

3 tablespoons Cognac or other brandy

½ cup (4 fl oz/125 ml) heavy (double) cream

¼ cup (2 fl oz/60 ml) veal demi-glace (page 53) or 1 cup (8 fl oz/250 ml) beef stock, reduced to ¼ cup

SKATE WINGS WITH
BROWN BUTTER AND CAPER SAUCE

4 skinless, boneless
skate wings, about 6 oz
(185 g) each

Salt and freshly ground
pepper

About 1 cup (5 oz/155 g)
all-purpose (plain) flour

2 teaspoons canola oil

FOR THE BROWN BUTTER
SAUCE:

⅓ cup (3 oz/90 g)
unsalted butter, at room
temperature, plus
2 tablespoons chilled
unsalted butter,
cut into 4 pieces

¼ cup (2 oz/60 g) capers,
preferably salt-packed,
rinsed

2 tablespoons good-quality
balsamic vinegar

2 tablespoons minced
fresh flat-leaf (Italian)
parsley

¼ –½ teaspoon fresh
lemon juice

Place a large baking dish in the oven and preheat to 150°F (65°C).

Pat the skate wings dry with paper towels and season both sides with salt and pepper. Put the flour in a shallow bowl.

In a large frying pan over medium-high heat, heat the oil (or use 2 pans if necessary to avoid overcrowding, making the sauce in one of the pans). Dredge the skate wings in the flour, shaking off the excess, and add them to the pan. Sauté, carefully turning once, until firm and golden brown, about 5 minutes on each side. Transfer to the platter in the oven.

To make the brown butter sauce, wipe out the pan with a paper towel and return the heat to medium. Melt the ⅓ cup butter in the pan. As soon as it begins to turn dark brown (don't let it burn), remove the pan from the heat and carefully add the capers and vinegar (they will splatter). Add the 2 tablespoons butter and the parsley and swirl the pan just until the butter melts and the sauce is slightly thickened. Stir in ¼ teaspoon lemon juice and taste for acidity; add the remaining juice if desired.

Drizzle the sauce over the skate wings and serve at once.

Variation Tip: If skate wings are unavailable, substitute 16 large scallops, preferably dry-packed. Dredge in flour as described above, and sear, turning once, until the scallops are firm and just losing translucence around the center, 2–2½ minutes on each side.

MAKES 4 SERVINGS

BROWN BUTTER

Brown butter, known in French as *beurre noisette* ("hazelnut butter"), is simply melted butter that is cooked until it turns nut brown and develops an intense flavor. The primary challenge in making it is in knowing when to halt the cooking. If it is cooked too long, the butter will burn and become bitter. To stop the cooking quickly, keep a wide bowl of cold water by the stove, and immerse the base of the pan in it when the butter has reached the ideal shade of nut brown.

PORK CHOPS WITH PORT AND DRIED CHERRY SAUCE

Place a large baking dish in the oven and preheat to 150°F (65°C).

Pat the pork chops dry with paper towels and season both sides generously with salt and pepper. Using a sieve or sifter, dust both sides lightly with flour.

In a large frying pan over medium-high heat, heat the oil (use 2 pans if necessary to avoid crowding; make the sauce in one of the pans). When the oil just begins to smoke, add the chops and cook, without moving them, for 2½ minutes. Turn the chops over and cook until firm to the touch and golden, about 2½ minutes longer. Transfer the chops to the baking dish in the oven.

Return the pan to medium heat and make the Port and dried cherry sauce: Carefully add the Port and cherries to the pan (they will splatter). Bring to a simmer and deglaze the pan, scraping up the browned bits from the bottom and sides, and cook until the liquid is reduced by half, about 2 minutes. Add the stock, vinegar, rosemary, ¼ teaspoon salt, and a pinch of pepper and simmer until the sauce is slightly syrupy, about 2 minutes. Taste and adjust the seasoning. Remove the pan from the heat. Add the butter, if using, and swirl the pan until the butter melts and the sauce is slightly thickened, about 30 seconds.

Transfer the chops to warmed individual plates. Top each with a spoonful of the sauce and serve at once.

MAKES 4 SERVINGS

REDUCTIONS
You can reduce any liquid simply by simmering it briskly. Doing this will decrease the volume through evaporation, concentrate the flavor, and thicken the consistency. The longer you reduce a liquid, the deeper the flavor and the thicker the consistency. The resulting sauce is commonly called a reduction. Because flavors will be magnified by this process, it is best to use high-quality ingredients.

4 boneless pork loin or center-cut chops, 6–7 oz (185–220 g) each

Salt and freshly ground pepper

All-purpose (plain) flour for dusting

2 teaspoons canola or vegetable oil

FOR THE PORT AND DRIED CHERRY SAUCE:

1 cup (8 fl oz/250 ml) ruby Port

⅔ cup (3 oz/90 g) dried cherries or cranberries, soaked in water for 20 minutes and drained

½ cup (4 fl oz/125 ml) chicken stock (page 112) or prepared broth

¼ teaspoon red wine vinegar

1 teaspoon minced fresh rosemary

Salt and freshly ground pepper

2 tablespoons unsalted butter, cut into 4 pieces (optional)

PASTA SAUCES

The Italians have elevated saucing a bowl of pasta to an art: consider the bright, herbal flavor of a well-made pesto when paired with delicate angel hair, or the comforting creaminess of fettuccine Alfredo. A classic ragù *typically simmers for hours to achieve its maximum flavor, but most pasta sauces can be made quickly and with minimal effort.*

GNOCCHI ALLA ROMANA
WITH CLASSIC TOMATO SAUCE
62

BUCATINI WITH AMATRICIANA SAUCE
65

ANGEL HAIR PASTA WITH PESTO
66

FETTUCCINE ALFREDO
69

RUOTE WITH TOMATO, BASIL,
AND FRESH MOZZARELLA
70

LINGUINE WITH LOBSTER-TARRAGON SAUCE
73

FRESH PAPPARDELLE WITH RAGÙ
74

GNOCCHI ALLA ROMANA
WITH CLASSIC TOMATO SAUCE

PEELING AND SEEDING TOMATOES
To peel and seed tomatoes, first cut a shallow X in the bottom of each tomato. Immerse the tomatoes in boiling water for 20 seconds, then plunge them into cold water. Starting at the X, peel off the skin with your fingers or a paring knife. (Peaches can be peeled by the same method.) Cut in half crosswise and squeeze to dislodge the seeds. If flavorful fresh tomatoes are unavailable for this recipe, canned whole plum (Roma) tomatoes make a fine substitute.

To make the gnocchi, in a saucepan over medium-high heat, combine the milk, 1½ cups (12 fl oz/375 ml) water, the butter, ½ teaspoon salt, and ¼ teaspoon white pepper and bring to a boil. Reduce the heat to medium-low and slowly pour in the semolina flour in a thin stream, whisking until no lumps remain. Reduce the heat to low and cook, stirring, until thick, about 8 minutes. Add the ½ cup Parmesan cheese and sage. Remove from the heat. Transfer the semolina mixture to a dampened baking sheet. Using a spatula, spread the mixture in an even layer about ½ inch (12 mm) thick. Cover with a kitchen towel and let stand for at least 1 hour at room temperature, or refrigerate overnight.

To make the sauce, in a large frying pan over medium-high heat, heat the oil. Add the garlic and sauté until golden, 1–2 minutes. Add the tomatoes with juice and crush with a wooden spoon. Bring to a boil, then reduce the heat to medium. Add the wine, ½ teaspoon salt, and a pinch of black pepper and simmer for 15 minutes. Remove from the heat and let stand for 5 minutes. Discard the garlic. Pass the sauce through a food mill or purée in a food processor. Add the basil just before assembling the dish.

Preheat the oven to 400°F (200°C). Lightly oil a 10-inch (25-cm) round baking dish. Using a 3-inch (7.5-cm) round cookie cutter, cut out as many gnocchi as possible. Arrange them in a circle in a single layer in the prepared baking dish, overlapping them by half and leaving a small space in the center. Sprinkle with the ¼ cup Parmesan. Drizzle the sauce around the edges of the dish and in the center; do not cover the gnocchi completely with sauce.

Bake until the cheese is melted and slightly golden and the sauce is bubbling, 20–25 minutes. Let stand for 5 minutes, then serve.

MAKES 6 SERVINGS

FOR THE GNOCCHI:

1½ cups (12 fl oz/375 ml) whole milk

3 tablespoons unsalted butter

Salt and freshly ground white pepper

¾ cup (4 oz/125 g) semolina flour (page 115)

½ cup (2 oz/60 g) grated Parmesan cheese

2 teaspoons minced fresh sage

FOR THE TOMATO SAUCE:

1 tablespoon extra-virgin olive oil

1 clove garlic, crushed

1½ lb (750 g) ripe plum (Roma) tomatoes, peeled and seeded *(far left)*, or 2 cups (16 oz/500 g) canned tomatoes with juice

2 tablespoons dry white wine or vermouth

Salt and freshly ground black pepper

1 tablespoon shredded fresh basil

¼ cup (1 oz/30 g) grated Parmesan cheese

BUCATINI WITH AMATRICIANA SAUCE

FOR THE SAUCE:

1 tablespoon extra-virgin olive oil

2 oz (60 g) pancetta, chopped

½ white or yellow onion, finely chopped

½ teaspoon red pepper flakes

⅔ cup (5 fl oz/160 ml) dry red wine

2 cups (16 oz/500 g) canned tomatoes with juice or 1½ lb (750 g) plum (Roma) tomatoes, peeled, seeded (page 62), and diced

Salt and freshly ground black pepper

3 fresh basil leaves, finely chopped

2 teaspoons minced fresh flat-leaf (Italian) parsley

2 tablespoons grated pecorino romano cheese, plus more, shaved, for serving

Kosher salt

1 lb (500 g) bucatini or spaghetti

In a frying pan over medium-low heat, heat the oil. Add the pancetta and sauté until lightly golden, 2–3 minutes. Add the onion and red pepper flakes and cook, stirring occasionally, until the onion is soft, 5–6 minutes. Add the wine and simmer until it is almost completely evaporated, about 1½ minutes.

Add the tomatoes and their juice and crush with a wooden spoon. Bring to a gentle simmer and cook, uncovered, until slightly thickened, about 10 minutes. Stir in ½ teaspoon salt and a pinch of black pepper. Remove the sauce from the heat and stir in the basil, parsley, and grated cheese. Season to taste with salt and black pepper, then cover the pan.

Meanwhile, bring a large saucepan three-fourths full of water to a rapid boil over high heat. Add 1 tablespoon kosher salt and the pasta and cook until al dente. Drain the pasta and put it in a large warmed serving bowl. Add the sauce and toss to coat the pasta evenly. Divide the pasta among warmed individual plates and top each serving with a few shavings of cheese. Serve at once.

MAKES 4 SERVINGS

AMATRICIANA SAUCE

In Italy, this simple sauce, which is particularly popular in Rome, is made with *guanciale* (cured pork cheek), but pancetta is an excellent substitute. The sauce originated in Amatrice, a town in Lazio near the border with Abruzzo. It is typically tossed with bucatini, which is similar to spaghetti, but slightly stouter, with a hollow center. Amatriciana is usually served with with pecorino romano cheese, but Parmesan is equally good.

ANGEL HAIR PASTA WITH PESTO

To make the pesto, in a small dry frying pan over medium heat, toast the pine nuts, shaking the pan frequently, until pale gold, about 2 minutes. Transfer the nuts to a plate and let cool.

Bring a small saucepan three-fourths full of water to a boil over high heat. Add the basil, pressing down with a spoon to immerse the leaves, then immediately drain in a colander. Scrape the leaves into a bowl of ice water, stir, and let cool for 3 minutes, then drain again. Squeeze small handfuls of the basil to extract as much water as possible and chop coarsely.

In a mortar, combine the pine nuts, garlic, and about 1 teaspoon salt. Using a pestle, pound into a smooth paste. Add half of the basil and pound into a paste, then add the remaining basil and pound until fairly smooth. Add the spinach and ¼ teaspoon pepper and pound until incorporated. Add the olive oil 2 tablespoons at a time, pounding and scraping down the sides of the mortar until a smooth paste forms; add the lemon juice to the mixture and stir. (This can also be done in a mini food processor.) Transfer to a nonreactive bowl and fold in the cheese.

Meanwhile, bring a large saucepan three-fourths full of water to a rapid boil over high heat. Add 1 tablespoon kosher salt and the pasta and cook until al dente. Drain the pasta, reserving ¼ cup (2 fl oz/60 ml) of the cooking water. Put the pasta in a warmed serving bowl. Add the pesto and the reserved water and toss to coat the pasta evenly. Serve at once, and pass the grated Parmesan at the table.

Variation Tip: Variations on classic pesto—such as this recipe, which adds baby spinach to the mix—abound: Substitute parsley or arugula (rocket) for half of the basil, replace the pine nuts with walnuts, or adjust the amount of garlic to your personal taste.

MAKES 4 SERVINGS

BASIL

Once a hard-to-find seasonal commodity, fresh basil is now available year-round. This aromatic herb tends to become bitter as the plant matures: the smaller, younger leaves are milder and only slightly peppery, while the larger leaves can overwhelm a sauce with their pungency. Blanching the leaves before combining them with other ingredients will help keep your pesto a lovely emerald green.

FOR THE PESTO:

2 tablespoons pine nuts

1½ cups (3 oz/90 g) firmly packed fresh basil leaves

2 large cloves garlic, minced

Salt and freshly ground pepper

½ cup (½ oz/15 g) baby spinach, stems removed and leaves coarsely chopped

½ cup (4 fl oz/125 ml) extra-virgin olive oil

1 tablespoon fresh lemon juice

⅓ cup (1½ oz/45 g) grated Parmesan or grana padano cheese

Kosher salt

1 lb (500 g) angel hair pasta

Grated Parmesan or grana padano cheese for serving

FETTUCCINE ALFREDO

1 cup (8 fl oz/250 ml) heavy (double) cream

2 tablespoons unsalted butter

Kosher salt

1 pound (500 g) dried fettuccine

Salt and freshly ground white pepper

Tiny pinch of freshly grated nutmeg

1 cup (4 oz/125 g) grated Parmesan or grana padano cheese

Bring a large saucepan three-fourths full of water to a rapid boil.

In a large frying pan over medium heat, combine the cream and the butter. Bring to a boil, then reduce the heat to medium-low and simmer, swirling the pan occasionally, until slightly thickened, about 1 minute. Remove from the heat.

Once the water is boiling, add 1 tablespoon kosher salt and the pasta and cook until almost al dente. Drain the pasta well, shaking off the excess water. Add the pasta to the sauce and set it over low heat. Toss to coat the pasta evenly and add ½ teaspoon salt, ⅛ teaspoon white pepper, and the nutmeg. Simmer, stirring and tossing, until the noodles have absorbed most of the sauce, 1–2 minutes. Remove from the heat and add ¾ cup (3 oz/90 g) of the cheese, tossing until the cheese melts and coats the pasta evenly. Sprinkle with the remaining ¼ cup (1 oz/30 g) cheese.

Divide among warmed individual plates and serve at once.

MAKES 4 SERVINGS

ALFREDO SAUCE

This simple mixture of cream, butter, and cheese owes its name to Roman chef Alfredo Di Lelio, who served the now-legendary sauce to the honeymooning Douglas Fairbanks and Mary Pickford in 1920. They reportedly ate it every night of their Roman visit and then sang its praises once they returned to Hollywood. Good-quality ingredients are the key to the sauce's success. Parmesan cheese varies greatly; imported Parmigiano-Reggiano is the best choice. Grana padano, a similar aged cheese from northern Italy, is an excellent alternative.

RUOTE WITH TOMATO, BASIL, AND FRESH MOZZARELLA

In a large, wide nonreactive bowl, combine the tomatoes and any juices from the cutting board, the garlic, basil, 1½ teaspoons salt, a pinch of pepper, the cheese, and olive oil and stir to combine. Cover with plastic wrap and let stand at room temperature for 2 hours to allow the flavors to marry.

Bring a large saucepan three-fourths full of water to a rapid boil over high heat. Add 1 tablespoon kosher salt and the pasta and cook until al dente. Reserve ¼ cup (2 fl oz/60 ml) of the cooking water. Drain the pasta, add it to the sauce in the bowl, and toss to coat the pasta evenly (do not let stand before tossing, or the cheese may melt together into large lumps). Add the reserved cooking water and stir. Drizzle with the balsamic vinegar and serve at once in warmed individual bowls.

Note: Ruote is a type of dried pasta shaped like wagon wheels that pairs well with chunky sauces. Other shapes, like penne, farfalle, or fusilli, may be substituted.

MAKES 4 SERVINGS

FRESH MOZZARELLA

The pride of southern Italy's Campania region, mozzarella is a fresh cheese, made by immersing curds in hot water and then kneading and molding them into balls by hand. The balls are then sold packed in whey or water. *Mozzarella di bufala*, made from the milk of water buffaloes, is the finest mozzarella, but fresh cow's milk mozzarella, made in Italy and elsewhere, is a good substitute. This cheese is highly perishable, however, so use it as soon as possible after purchase.

1½ lb (750 g) ripe plum (Roma) tomatoes, peeled and seeded (page 62), then diced

2 cloves garlic, minced

10–15 fresh basil leaves, torn into small pieces

Salt and freshly ground pepper

½ lb (250 g) fresh mozzarella cheese, diced

⅔ cup (5 fl oz/160 ml) extra-virgin olive oil

Kosher salt

1 lb (500 g) ruote pasta (see Note)

1 teaspoon aged balsamic vinegar

LINGUINE WITH LOBSTER-TARRAGON SAUCE

1 lobster shell *(far right)*

3 tablespoons unsalted butter

2 small shallots, coarsely chopped

1 small carrot, peeled and coarsely chopped

1 small leek, white part only, coarsely chopped

½ teaspoon tomato paste

1 bay leaf

1 fresh thyme sprig

2 fresh tarragon sprigs

Salt and freshly ground white pepper

2 teaspoons Cognac

¾ cup (6 fl oz/180 ml) dry white wine or vermouth

2 cups (16 fl oz/500 ml) heavy (double) cream

2 teaspoons unsalted butter

6 oz (185 g) cooked lobster meat, coarsely chopped

Kosher salt

1 lb (500 g) dried linguine

1 tablespoon minced fresh tarragon

To make the sauce, put the lobster shell in a plastic bag and smash with a meat mallet or a rolling pin.

In a large frying pan over medium-high heat, melt the 3 tablespoons butter. Add the lobster shell pieces and sauté, stirring frequently, until golden brown and aromatic, 2–3 minutes. Add the shallots, carrot, leek, tomato paste, bay leaf, and thyme and tarragon sprigs and reduce the heat to medium. Sauté, stirring frequently, for 2 minutes. Season with salt and white pepper.

Add the Cognac and cook for 1 minute. Add the wine and cook, stirring occasionally, until it is almost completely evaporated, about 8 minutes. Stir in the cream, ¾ teaspoon salt, and ¼ teaspoon white pepper. Bring to a simmer, then reduce the heat to low and simmer, uncovered, stirring occasionally, until slightly thickened, about 15 minutes. Strain through a fine-mesh sieve into a bowl or measuring pitcher, pressing down on the solids to extract all of the sauce. Wipe out the pan with a paper towel to remove any bits of shell and return the sauce to the pan. Taste and adjust the seasoning, and set aside for up to 20 minutes. Reheat gently just before serving.

In a small frying pan over low heat, melt the 2 tablespoons butter. Add the lobster meat and cook, stirring occasionally, until warmed through, 3 minutes. Remove from the heat; keep warm.

Meanwhile, bring a large saucepan three-fourths full of water to a rapid boil over high heat. Add 1 tablespoon kosher salt and the pasta and cook until al dente. Drain the pasta, add it to the sauce, and toss to coat the pasta evenly. Add half of the minced tarragon and toss again. Transfer to a large warmed bowl and scatter the lobster meat and the remaining tarragon on top. Serve at once.

MAKES 4 SERVINGS

WORKING WITH LOBSTER

In order to make the most flavorful lobster sauce, start with an empty lobster shell. The shell imparts great flavor and color to a sauce, even after the meat has been removed. The next time you cook lobster or order one at a restaurant, save the shell and store it in the freezer. Seafood markets may also have empty shells on hand. In the absence of a lobster shell, you can use 6 oz (185 g) shrimp (prawns) in the shell, chopped coarsely with their shells on.

FRESH PAPPARDELLE WITH RAGÙ

To make the *ragù*, in a large, heavy Dutch oven over medium-low heat, heat the olive oil. Add the onion, carrot, and celery and cook, stirring occasionally, until the onion is golden, about 10 minutes. Add the garlic and bay leaves and cook for 1 minute. Add the beef and pork and cook, stirring to break up any chunks, until the beef is no longer pink, about 7 minutes. Add the wine, raise the heat to high, and cook until slightly reduced, about 5 minutes. Add the diced tomatoes, tomato purée, and cream; stir to combine. Reduce the heat to low, cover partially, and cook, stirring occasionally, until the flavors have melded and the sauce is thickened and slightly reduced, 1½ hours or more. Stir in ¾ teaspoon salt and ¼ teaspoon pepper and cook for 10 minutes longer. Discard the bay leaves. Taste and adjust the seasoning, then stir in the basil.

About 10 minutes before the sauce is ready, bring a large saucepan three-fourths full of water to a rapid boil. Add 1 tablespoon kosher salt and the pasta to the water and cook for about 1½–2 minutes for homemade pasta, a little longer for purchased fresh pasta.

Put 2 cups (16 fl oz/500 ml) of the sauce into a large warmed serving bowl. Drain the pasta and add it to the bowl. Toss to coat all the pasta evenly and sprinkle with the ½ cup Parmesan cheese. Spoon more sauce on top and serve at once. Pass additional cheese at the table.

MAKES 6 SERVINGS

SOFFRITTO

Every Italian *ragù* (meat sauce) typically begins with a *soffritto,* a mixture of onion, carrot, and celery sautéed in olive oil. (In French cooking, this triad is called *mirepoix.*) Sometimes a *soffritto* also includes garlic, parsley, and/or prosciutto or pancetta, and it can be the base not only for *ragù,* but for countless other Italian sauces, braises, and soups as well. When making a *ragù*, it is important to cook the *soffritto* over moderate heat, long enough for the vegetables to soften.

FOR THE RAGÙ:

3 tablespoons extra-virgin olive oil

1 *each* small white onion, carrot, and celery stalk, finely chopped

2 cloves garlic, minced

2 bay leaves

½ lb (250 g) *each* ground (minced) beef and ground (minced) pork or veal

1 cup (8 fl oz/250 ml) full-bodied red wine

One 14-oz (440-g) can diced plum (Roma) tomatoes with juice

One 14-oz (440 g) can tomato purée

¾ cup (6 fl oz/180 ml) heavy (double) cream

Salt and freshly ground pepper

8 large fresh basil leaves, cut into narrow strips

Kosher salt

1¼ lb (625 g) fresh pappardelle, homemade (page 113) or purchased

½ cup (2 oz/60 g) grated Parmesan cheese, plus more for serving

SALSAS, PURÉES, AND RELISHES

Salsas originated in Latin America, and the Mexican classic, salsa fresca, *may be the most popular and versatile of them all. Argentina's piquant* chimichurri *and Cuban* mojo *both add zip and spice to roast meats, while* romesco, *the Spanish purée that features almonds and peppers, is a savory contrast to fried fish.*

CHEESE QUESADILLAS WITH SALSA FRESCA
78

ROAST PORK LOIN WITH
RED ONION, PARSLEY, AND ORANGE MOJO
81

GRILLED MAHIMAHI
WITH PINEAPPLE-TEQUILA SALSA
82

FRIED CALAMARI WITH ROMESCO
85

GRILLED FLANK STEAK WITH CHIMICHURRI
86

DUCK BREAST WITH PEACH AND MANGO SALSA
89

CHEESE QUESADILLAS WITH SALSA FRESCA

CHILE VARIETIES

Today you can find a wide range of fresh chiles in supermarkets and specialty stores. The long, gently tapered Anaheim is mild and most suitable for stuffing; the broader, shorter poblano is hotter and is always used cooked or roasted rather than eaten raw. Of the hotter chiles, the bright green jalapeño is the mildest, while the serrano is quite fiery. The small, slender Thai chile is about three times hotter than the serrano, and habanero chiles can be incendiary. (See page 24 for instructions on working with chiles.)

To make the salsa, seed the tomatoes as directed on page 62 but do not peel. Cut into ¼-inch (6-mm) dice. In a nonreactive bowl, combine the tomatoes, red onion, chile, chopped cilantro, lime juice, ½ teaspoon salt, and a pinch of pepper and stir to blend. The salsa is best when served immediately, but it may be covered and refrigerated for up to 6 hours.

Place a large ovenproof platter in the oven and preheat to 150°F (65°C). To make the quesadillas, set a large nonstick frying pan over medium-low heat. Put a tortilla in the pan and sprinkle evenly with ½ cup (2 oz/60 g) of the cheese mixture, leaving a ½-inch (12-mm) border uncovered. Sprinkle evenly with one-fourth of the green onions, season generously with salt and pepper, and sprinkle with 1 teaspoon of the Tabasco, if using. Sprinkle with another ½ cup of the cheese and top with a second tortilla. Cook, pressing down with a spatula occasionally, until the cheese begins to melt, about 2 minutes. Carefully turn the quesadilla over and cook until a little melted cheese appears around the edges, about 1 minute longer. Transfer to the platter in the oven. Repeat with the remaining tortillas and other ingredients to make 4 quesadillas in all.

Using a large knife or a pizza wheel, cut each quesadilla into quarters and top each wedge with a generous spoonful of salsa and a dollop of sour cream. Garnish with cilantro sprigs and serve at once.

Variation Tip: There are many variations on the classic salsa fresca. Try substituting any soft fruit for the tomatoes; green onions or shallots for the red onion; or parsley for the cilantro.

MAKES 4 SERVINGS

FOR THE SALSA:

3 plum (Roma) tomatoes

3 tablespoons finely diced red onion

1 jalapeño chile, seeded and finely chopped

½ cup (½ oz/15 g) fresh cilantro (fresh coriander) leaves, coarsely chopped

1 tablespoon fresh lime juice

Salt and freshly ground pepper

FOR THE QUESADILLAS:

8 flour tortillas, 8 inches (20 cm) in diameter

1⅓ cups (5 oz/155 g) *each* shredded Monterey jack, white Cheddar, and smoked Mozzarella cheese

4 green (spring) onions, including tender green parts, very thinly sliced

Salt and freshly ground pepper

4 teaspoons Tabasco sauce (optional)

1 cup (8 oz/250 g) sour cream

ROAST PORK LOIN WITH
RED ONION, PARSLEY, AND ORANGE MOJO

¼ cup (2 fl oz/60 ml) medium-dry or dry sherry

¼ cup (2½ oz/75 g) orange marmalade

Double boneless pork loin, 4–6 lb (2–3 kg), about 4½ inches (11.5 cm) in diameter (see Note)

Salt and freshly ground pepper

FOR THE MOJO:

1 small red onion, finely chopped

Zest of 2 oranges, finely chopped

½ cup (4 fl oz/125 ml) fresh orange juice

¼ cup (2 fl oz/60 ml) fresh lime juice

6 cloves garlic, minced

Salt and freshly ground pepper

¾ cup (1 oz/30 g) minced fresh flat-leaf (Italian) parsley

¾ cup (6 fl oz/180 ml) extra-virgin olive oil

In a small saucepan over medium-high heat, combine the sherry and marmalade and cook, whisking constantly, until the mixture just reaches a simmer, about 2 minutes. Remove from the heat, cover, and set aside.

Trim the pork loin of excess fat, shape it into a cylinder, and tie with kitchen string. Put the pork on a rack in a roasting pan. Brush the pork on all sides with some of the sherry mixture and season generously with salt and pepper. Cover with plastic wrap and let stand at room temperature for about 1 hour.

Meanwhile, make the *mojo:* In a nonreactive bowl, combine the onion, orange zest, orange and lime juices, garlic, 1¼ teaspoons salt, ¾ teaspoon pepper, the parsley, and olive oil and stir. Cover and refrigerate until ready to use, for up to 12 hours. Bring to room temperature before serving.

Preheat the oven to 400°F (200°C). Brush the pork with a little more of the sherry mixture. Roast for 25 minutes, then reduce the oven temperature to 325°F (165°C). Continue to roast, basting occasionally with the remaining sherry mixture, until an instant-read thermometer inserted into the thickest part of the roast registers 150°F (65°C), about 1 hour and 20 minutes longer. (Timing will depend on the thickness, not the weight; a roast with a small diameter will cook more quickly.)

Transfer the pork to a rack, tent loosely with aluminum foil, and let rest for 10 minutes. Transfer to a board and carve into slices ½–¾ inch (12 mm–2 cm) thick. Serve on warmed individual plates with the *mojo* spooned on top.

Note: Double pork loin is made by tying two loins together. It takes longer to cook than a single loin, but stays moist.

MAKES 8–12 SERVINGS

WHAT IS MOJO?

Mojo (pronounced *mo-ho*) is a Cuban sauce that may be served hot or cold. It typically contains olive oil, fresh citrus juice, garlic, chopped fresh herbs, and aromatic seasonings, often cumin. It may also include diced shallots or onions, and occasionally butter replaces some of the olive oil. It is used as a marinade, a table sauce, and a dip, and is a traditional accompaniment to suckling pig and roasted or grilled vegetables.

GRILLED MAHIMAHI
WITH PINEAPPLE-TEQUILA SALSA

To make the salsa, in a nonreactive bowl, combine the pineapple, bell pepper, onion, chipotle chile, tequila, ¼ teaspoon salt, mint, and cilantro and stir. Cover and refrigerate for up to 4 hours to allow the flavors to marry.

Prepare a charcoal or gas grill for direct grilling over medium heat.

Brush both sides of the mahimahi fillets with the oil and season them generously with salt and pepper. Grill the fillets, without moving them, for 3 minutes. Using a metal spatula, carefully turn them over, keeping the golden crust intact. Grill, without moving them, until firm to the touch and just opaque through to the center, 1½–2 minutes longer.

Transfer the steaks to warmed individual plates and let rest for 1–2 minutes. Top with a spoonful of the salsa and serve at once.

Note: Canned chiles chipotle en adobo *are available in well-stocked markets and Mexican groceries. Once opened, they can be kept refrigerated in a covered glass or plastic container. You may also substitute ¼ teaspoon ground chipotle chile for the canned chile.*

MAKES 4 SERVINGS

TEQUILA

Tequila is made from the distilled juice of the blue agave, a close relative of the century plant. There are three basic types: *Blanco*, also known as silver or white tequila, can legally go directly from the still to the bottle, but is often left to settle first for a few weeks in steel vats.

Gold tequila is *blanco* to which caramel coloring has been added. *Reposado* tequila must spend 2 to 12 weeks in wooden casks, while the more refined *añejo* spends at least a year in wood and typically longer.

FOR THE SALSA:

¾ cup (4½ oz/140 g) finely diced fresh pineapple (¼-inch/6-mm dice), or 1 can (5½ oz/170 g) pineapple rings, drained and diced

½ large red bell pepper (capsicum), finely diced

1 tablespoon finely chopped white onion

1 teaspoon finely chopped canned *chile chipotle en adobo*, sauce scraped away (see Note)

1½ teaspoons tequila *(far left),* preferably *añejo*

Salt

6 fresh mint leaves, minced

1 teaspoon minced fresh cilantro (fresh coriander)

4 mahimahi steaks, each 6–7 oz (185–220 g) and about 1½ inches (4 cm) thick

1 tablespoon canola or vegetable oil

Salt and freshly ground pepper

FRIED CALAMARI WITH ROMESCO

1 lb (500 g) fresh or thawed frozen calamari (squid), cut into ½-inch (12-mm) rings, tentacles left intact

1 cup (8 fl oz/250 ml) whole milk

Salt and freshly ground black pepper

Romesco Sauce for serving *(far right)*

Vegetable or canola oil for deep-frying

1 cup (5 oz/155 g) rice flour or all-purpose (plain) flour

½ cup (2½ oz/75 g) coarse yellow cornmeal or polenta

1 tablespoon paprika

⅛ teaspoon cayenne pepper, or to taste

Minced fresh flat-leaf (Italian) parsley for garnish (optional)

In a bowl, combine the calamari, milk, and a pinch *each* of salt and black pepper. Cover and refrigerate for 1–4 hours. Meanwhile, make the *romesco (right)*.

Place an ovenproof platter in the oven and preheat to 150°F (65°C). Pour oil to a depth of 2 inches (5 cm) into a heavy, deep frying pan or wide saucepan and heat to 375°F (190°C) on a deep-frying thermometer.

While the oil heats, drain the calamari. In a large bowl, combine the rice flour, cornmeal, paprika, cayenne, 1 teaspoon salt, and ¼ teaspoon black pepper. Add half of the calamari and toss to coat evenly, then transfer the coated calamari to a colander and shake gently to remove excess flour.

Add the coated calamari to the hot oil and deep-fry, using a wire skimmer or slotted spoon to push it gently into the oil occasionally, until crisp and golden brown, about 1 minute. Using the skimmer or spoon, transfer to paper towels to drain briefly, then place on the platter in the oven. Coat the remaining calamari and fry in the same way.

Garnish the calamari with the parsley, if using, and place a small bowl or ramekin holding the *romesco* in the center of the platter. Serve at once.

Note: Romesco originated in Tarragona, in the Catalan region of Spain, and is traditionally served with grilled, poached, or deep-fried fish.

MAKES 4 SERVINGS

ROMESCO SAUCE

In a bowl, combine 1 oz (30 g) French bread chunks (about 2 slices), crusts removed, with 3 tablespoons red wine vinegar. Put ⅓ cup (1½ oz/45 g) toasted almonds in a food processor and pulse until grainy. Add the bread-vinegar mixture; ¼ cup (1½ oz/45 g) drained diced tomatoes; 1 roasted red pepper (capsicum; page 41), sliced; 1 clove garlic; 1 teaspoon paprika; and a pinch of cayenne. Purée until smooth. With the motor running, add ¼ cup (2 fl oz/60 ml) olive oil in a steady stream until smooth. Season to taste with salt and pepper and refrigerate for 1 hour.

GRILLED FLANK STEAK WITH CHIMICHURRI

CHIMICHURRI

In Argentina, the condiment *chimichurri* is ubiquitous—much like ketchup in the United States or soy sauce in China. It is served with nearly anything that is fried, grilled, or roasted, and is a must with the mixed-meat grill known as *asado* and with fried empanadas. It can also be used as a marinade. The texture ranges from smooth to chunky, and the ingredients vary as well, but the constants are olive oil, vinegar or lemon juice, garlic, and herbs.

Pat the flank steak dry with paper towels and place in a large baking dish. Brush both sides with the olive oil and season both sides generously with salt and pepper. Cover with plastic wrap and refrigerate for 4 hours or up to overnight. Let the steak come to room temperature for about 45 minutes before grilling.

To make the *chimichurri*, on a cutting board, finely chop the parsley, garlic, and oregano (this step can also be done in a food processor). Transfer the mixture to a small bowl and stir in the olive oil, 1 tablespoon sea salt, 1 teaspoon black pepper, and the red pepper flakes. If not using right away, you can cover the *chimichurri* and refrigerate until ready to use, for up to 4 hours; allow it to come to room temperature before using. Just before serving, stir in the vinegar.

Prepare a charcoal or gas grill for direct grilling over high heat. Grill the steak, without moving it, for 4 minutes. Turn it over and grill for 4–6 minutes longer for medium-rare, or longer if desired.

Transfer the steak to a carving board and tent loosely with aluminum foil, and let rest for 5 minutes. Cut diagonally across the grain into slices ¼ inch (6 mm) thick. Divide among warmed individual plates and top each serving with a generous spoonful of the *chimichurri*. Pass the remaining sauce at the table.

MAKES 4 SERVINGS

1 flank steak, about 3 lb (1.5 kg)

2 tablespoons extra-virgin olive oil

Salt and freshly ground black pepper

FOR THE CHIMICHURRI:

1½ cups (3 oz/90 g) firmly packed fresh flat-leaf (Italian) parsley leaves and tender stems

6 cloves garlic, quartered

2 tablespoons fresh oregano leaves

¾ cup (6 fl oz/180 ml) extra-virgin olive oil

Coarse sea salt or kosher salt and freshly ground black pepper

¼ teaspoon red pepper flakes

3 tablespoons white wine vinegar

DUCK BREAST WITH PEACH AND MANGO SALSA

FOR THE SALSA:

1 peeled ripe peach, cut into ½-inch (12-mm) dice

½ peeled ripe mango *(far right),* cut into ½-inch (12-mm) dice

½ small serrano chile, seeded and finely chopped (about ½ teaspoon), or to taste

3 green (spring) onions, including tender green parts, thinly sliced

½ cup (½ oz/15 g) loosely packed fresh cilantro (fresh coriander) leaves, coarsely chopped

2 tablespoons diced red bell pepper (capsicum) (optional)

1½ tablespoons fresh lime juice

Salt

4 boneless duck breast halves, 6–7 oz (185–220 g) each, skin on

Salt and freshly ground pepper

2 teaspoons canola oil

To make the salsa, in a nonreactive bowl, combine the peach, mango, chile, green onions, cilantro, bell pepper, lime juice, and ½ teaspoon salt and stir to combine. Cover and refrigerate for at least 30 minutes or up to 1 hour to allow the flavors to marry.

Bring the duck breasts to room temperature for 30–60 minutes. Preheat the oven to 375°F (190°C). Using a sharp knife, score the duck skin in several places, being careful not to cut into the flesh. Generously season both sides of each breast with salt and pepper.

In a large, heavy ovenproof frying pan over medium-high heat, heat the oil. Add the duck breasts, skin side down. Cook, without moving or pressing down on them, for 5 minutes, tipping the pan and spooning off the rendered fat halfway through the cooking. The skin should be brown and crisp. Turn the duck breasts over and transfer the pan to the oven. Cook for about 5 minutes longer for medium-rare, about 8 minutes longer for medium. To check for doneness, make an incision with a sharp knife; the breast should be reddish pink for medium-rare and very pale pink for medium. Remember that they will continue to cook after you remove them from the heat. Transfer the duck breasts to a carving board, tent loosely with aluminum foil, and let rest for 5 minutes.

Slice the duck across the grain about ½ inch (12 mm) thick. Fan a sliced duck breast on each warmed individual plate and place a mound of salsa on the side. Serve at once.

MAKES 4 SERVINGS

PREPARING MANGO

Using a vegetable peeler, peel the mango. Stand it on one of its narrow sides and, using a large, sharp knife positioned just off-center, cut off all the flesh from one side of the large, wide, flat pit in a single large slice. Repeat on the other side of the pit. Cut the flesh as desired. There will be some flesh still attached to the pit, which makes for nice, though messy, nibbling.

DESSERT SAUCES

Sweet sauces are an easy way to add a touch of decadence to dessert. Crème anglaise lends panache to an apple soufflé, while a raspberry coulis gives a splash of contrasting color to a mango mousse. Caramel sauce can be tricky, but once you master the basic technique, you will want to make it often.

BANANA SPLITS WITH HOT FUDGE SAUCE
92

APPLE SOUFFLÉ WITH CRÈME ANGLAISE
95

CARAMEL SWIRL ICE CREAM
WITH CARAMEL SAUCE
96

ALMOND POUND CAKE
WITH APRICOT-GRAND MARNIER SAUCE
99

CRÊPES WITH DARK CHOCOLATE
AND FRANGELICO SAUCE
100

MANGO MOUSSE WITH RASPBERRY COULIS
103

FRESH BERRIES WITH ZABAGLIONE
104

BANANA SPLITS WITH HOT FUDGE SAUCE

VANILLA

The vanilla bean was first cultivated and processed by the Aztecs, who used it to flavor a drink that would later be known as chocolate. Of the world's vanilla beans, 75 percent come from Madagascar, with Tahitian and Mexican beans making up the rest. When time allows, it's always best to use vanilla beans, scraping all the flavorful seeds from the interior, but high-quality extract (essence) also delivers the distinctive sweet and complex flavor of the bean.

To make the hot fudge sauce, in a small, heavy saucepan, combine the cocoa with just enough of the boiling water to make a thick paste, whisking with a fork (if you add all the water at once, the lumps will be hard to break up). Add the remaining boiling water, whisking until the cocoa dissolves. Set the pan over low heat and add the butter. When it melts, stir with a wooden spoon, then stir in the sugar and corn syrup.

Slowly bring the mixture to a simmer, stirring occasionally; do not allow it to boil. When small bubbles form around the edges of the pan, simmer, without stirring, until glossy and thick, about 8 minutes. Remove from the heat. Using a clean spoon, stir in the vanilla. If not using right away, keep warm in a double boiler.

Arrange 3 scoops of ice cream in a line down the center of each of 4 chilled oblong dishes. Place 1 banana half, cut side in, on either side of the ice cream. Spoon a generous amount of the hot fudge sauce over the top and sprinkle with the almonds. Dollop with whipped cream. Top each serving with 3 maraschino cherries, drizzle with liqueur, if using, and serve at once.

Serving Tip: If you do not have oblong dishes, cut each banana half in half crosswise. Put the ice cream in chilled round bowls and surround each portion with 4 banana quarters.

Note: The hot fudge sauce may be prepared in advance. Let it cool to room temperature, then cover and refrigerate for up to 1 week. Reheat the sauce gently in a double boiler over barely simmering water before serving.

MAKES 4 SERVINGS

FOR THE HOT FUDGE SAUCE:

6 tablespoons (1 oz/30 g) cocoa powder

⅓ cup (3 fl oz/80 ml) boiling water

3 tablespoons unsalted butter, cut into 6 pieces

1 cup (8 oz/250 g) sugar

2 tablespoons light corn syrup

1 teaspoon vanilla extract (essence)

12 small scoops best-quality vanilla ice cream (3–4 pints/1.5–2 l)

4 ripe bananas, peeled and halved lengthwise

½ cup (2 oz/60 g) sliced (flaked) almonds

Sweetened whipped cream for serving

12 maraschino cherries, drained, or raspberries

Liqueur, such as Grand Marnier or Kahlúa, for drizzling (optional)

APPLE SOUFFLÉ WITH CRÈME ANGLAISE

FOR THE CRÈME ANGLAISE:

1 cup (8 fl oz/250 ml) whole milk

¾ cup (6 fl oz/180 ml) heavy (double) cream

1 vanilla bean, split lengthwise, or ½ teaspoon vanilla extract (essence)

⅓ cup (3 oz/90 g) sugar

4 large egg yolks

FOR THE SOUFFLÉ:

3 "eating" apples such as Fuji or Golden Delicious, peeled, cored, and cut into eighths

1 tablespoon dry white wine

1 teaspoon unsalted butter

2 teaspoons sugar plus ⅓ cup (3 oz/90 g)

6 large egg whites

Pinch of salt

¼ teaspoon fresh lemon juice

To make the crème anglaise, in a heavy saucepan, combine the milk and cream. Scrape the seeds from the vanilla bean into the pan, then add the pod. Set the pan over medium heat and bring just to a simmer. Remove from the heat, add the sugar, and stir to dissolve. Let cool for 30 minutes; discard the vanilla pod.

In a small bowl, whisk the egg yolks until blended. Return the milk mixture just to a boil over medium-high heat, then remove from the heat. Slowly whisk one-fourth of the milk mixture into the yolks. Pour the egg mixture into the pan, whisking until blended.

Return to medium-low heat and cook, stirring constantly, until the sauce is thick enough to coat the spoon *(right)*, 3–4 minutes; do not allow to boil. Transfer to a heatproof bowl and stir frequently until cooled to room temperature. If using vanilla extract, stir in now. Cover and refrigerate until ready to use, up to 2 days.

To make the soufflé, in a small saucepan over low heat, combine the apples, wine, and 1 tablespoon water. Cook, covered, until the apples are soft, about 20 minutes. Uncover and continue cooking until the liquid evaporates, 5 minutes longer. Let the mixture cool for 5 minutes, then purée in a food processor until smooth.

Preheat the oven to 400°F (200°C). Butter a 6-cup (48–fl oz/1.5-l) soufflé dish and dust it with the 2 teaspoons sugar.

In a large metal bowl, using an electric mixer, beat the egg whites until foamy. Add the salt and lemon juice and beat until soft peaks form. Slowly add the ⅓ cup sugar, beating until stiff peaks form. Using a rubber spatula, fold in the apple purée. Scoop the mixture into the dish, mounding a bit above the rim and flattening the top.

Bake until puffed and firm, 25–30 minutes. Serve at once on dessert plates with a spoonful of crème anglaise alongside.

MAKES 4–6 SERVINGS

CRÈME ANGLAISE

Like many sauces and desserts in the European tradition, crème anglaise is a type of custard known as a stirred custard (as it is not baked). Just as when making hollandaise or béarnaise, it is crucial to keep the egg yolks from getting too hot too quickly or the sauce will curdle. To judge when a stirred custard is done, use the "trail test": Hold up the wooden spoon used to stir the custard and quickly draw your fingertip across it. If no sauce drips across the trail for a few seconds, the sauce has reached the correct consistency.

CARAMEL SWIRL ICE CREAM WITH CARAMEL SAUCE

FOR THE CARAMEL SAUCE:

2 cups (1 lb/500 g) sugar

1 cup (8 fl oz/250 ml) heavy (double) cream

Pinch of salt

FOR THE ICE CREAM:

2 cups (16 fl oz/500 ml) heavy (double) cream

1 cup (8 fl oz/250 ml) whole milk

½ cup (4 oz/125 g) sugar

4 large egg yolks

½ teaspoon vanilla extract (essence)

To make the sauce, in a large saucepan over medium heat, combine the sugar and ½ cup (4 fl oz/125 ml) water and stir until the sugar dissolves. Raise the heat to medium-high and cook, without stirring, until large bubbles form. Continue cooking until the caramel begins to brown, 10–12 minutes. Continue cooking, swirling the pan occasionally but not stirring, until the color becomes a deep amber. Carefully add the cream in a thin stream, whisking constantly until the bubbles subside. Whisk in the salt. Let stand about 20 minutes, then divide the sauce in half and let cool. Cover and refrigerate for up to 4 days.

To make the ice cream, in a large saucepan over low heat, heat the cream, milk, and sugar, stirring until the sugar dissolves, then heat to just below a simmer. Remove from the heat. In a small bowl, whisk the egg yolks until blended. Slowly whisk in one-fourth of the cream mixture, then pour the egg mixture into the pan, whisking constantly until blended. Return to medium heat and cook, stirring constantly, until the custard coats the back of the spoon, 3–4 minutes; do not allow to boil. Stir in the vanilla, pour into a glass pitcher, and let cool, stirring occasionally. Cover and refrigerate for at least 4 hours or up to overnight.

One hour before churning the ice cream, remove half the caramel sauce from the refrigerator. Pour the custard into an ice-cream maker and freeze according to the manufacturer's instructions. When it is the texture of soft-serve ice cream, pour in the room-temperature caramel sauce and churn until distributed in thick swirls. Pack into a container and freeze until serving time.

Reheat the remaining caramel sauce in the top of a double boiler over hot water until warm but not hot. Serve the ice cream in chilled bowls with the warm sauce drizzled on top.

MAKES 4–6 SERVINGS

CARAMEL TIPS

When making caramel, place a pastry brush in a cup of cold water near the stove. Turn the handle of the pan away from you, so you won't bump it, splashing very hot liquid. Cook the sugar mixture without stirring or swirling the pan until the bubbles increase in size and begin to break more slowly. If sugar crystals form on the sides of the pan, brush down the crystals with the damp brush. Don't use too much water or the caramel will become diluted and take longer to turn golden.

ALMOND POUND CAKE WITH APRICOT–GRAND MARNIER SAUCE

FOR THE SAUCE:

7 oz (220 g) dried apricots, thinly sliced

2½ cups (20 fl oz/625 ml) fresh orange juice

½ teaspoon vanilla extract (essence)

3 tablespoons Grand Marnier

FOR THE CAKE:

1 cup (8 oz/250 g) unsalted butter, at room temperature, plus more for greasing

¾ cup (5½ oz/170 g) superfine (caster) sugar

¼ teaspoon salt

1 teaspoon vanilla extract (essence)

3 large whole eggs plus 3 egg yolks, at room temperature

1¼ cups (6½ oz/200 g) all-purpose (plain) flour

¾ cup (3 oz/90 g) ground almonds (page 114)

1 teaspoon baking powder

2 tablespoons slivered almonds

To make the sauce, in a saucepan over medium-high heat, combine the apricots and orange juice. Bring to a boil, then reduce the heat to medium-low and simmer gently, stirring occasionally, for 1 hour. Let cool for 10 minutes. Transfer half of the mixture to a blender or food processor and purée until smooth. Return to the pan, stir in the vanilla and Grand Marnier, and set aside.

To make the cake, preheat the oven to 350°F (180°C). Butter a 9-by-5-inch (23-by-13-cm) nonstick loaf pan, line the bottom with parchment (baking) paper, and rub with a little more butter.

In a bowl, using a stand mixer fitted with the whisk attachment or a heavy-duty handheld mixer at medium speed, beat together the butter, sugar, and salt until pale and fluffy, 8–10 minutes. Add the vanilla, then add the eggs and egg yolks one at a time, beating well after each addition (don't worry if the batter looks curdled). Using a wide-mesh sieve, sift in the flour, ground almonds, and baking powder and beat until smooth, scraping down the sides of the bowl as necessary.

Transfer the batter to the prepared pan. Bake for 25 minutes, then sprinkle the almonds over the top. Continue to bake until a toothpick inserted into the center comes out clean, about 25 minutes longer. Remove from the oven and let cool in the pan for 10 minutes. Run a knife around the inside edge of the pan to loosen the cake, turn the cake out onto one hand, and peel off the paper. Place right side up on wire rack and let cool completely. Cut the cake into thick slices and serve each with a large spoonful of the sauce.

MAKES 8 SERVINGS

ORANGE LIQUEURS

Grand Marnier is the grande dame of orange-flavored liqueurs, which also include Cointreau, Curaçao, Mandarine, and Triple Sec. Grand Marnier is made by flavoring brandy with bitter Haitian orange peel, vanilla, and spices. It is typically sipped over ice when not being used—always sparingly—in desserts and dessert sauces such as the one in this recipe.

CRÊPES WITH DARK CHOCOLATE
AND FRANGELICO SAUCE

DARK CHOCOLATE
Chocolate is produced
through a complex process
that includes fermenting,
drying, roasting, and shelling
cocoa beans to yield a
thick paste that is the base
for all types of chocolate.
Unsweetened, or "baking,"
chocolate is extremely
bitter. Most recipes call for
bittersweet chocolate, which
contains 35 percent pure
chocolate mass, or the slightly
sweeter semisweet (plain),
with 15 percent to 35 percent
chocolate mass. Chocolate
scorches easily, so it's best
to melt it in a double boiler.

To make the sauce, combine the milk, cream, and chocolate in the top pan of a double boiler set over (but not touching) barely simmering water in the bottom pan. (Alternatively, use a heat-proof bowl that fits snugly on top of a saucepan.) Heat, stirring frequently, until the chocolate melts and the mixture is smooth, 3–4 minutes. If serving right away, stir in the Frangelico. If not, let the sauce cool to room temperature, then cover and refrigerate for up to 2 days. Reheat gently in a double boiler and stir in the Frangelico just before serving.

Make the crêpes according to the instructions on page 113. To assemble the dish, in a large frying pan over low heat, melt 2 teaspoons of the butter. Place a finished crêpe with the attractive side (the side that was cooked first) down in the pan. Fold the crêpe in half, then in half again to form a triangle. Move the crêpe to the side of the pan and repeat with 3 more crêpes, adding more butter as necessary to keep them moist. Transfer the 4 crêpes to a warmed individual plate. Repeat with the remaining 12 crêpes, adding more butter as necessary, and putting 4 crêpes on each plate. Drizzle generously with the warm sauce, dust with confectioners' sugar, and serve at once.

Variation Tip: If you prefer, substitute Cognac or Grand Marnier for the Frangelico, an Italian liqueur flavored with hazelnuts (filberts).

MAKES 4 SERVINGS

FOR THE SAUCE:

¼ cup (2 fl oz/60 ml)
whole milk

¼ cup (2 fl oz/60 ml)
heavy (double) cream

¼ lb (125 g) **bittersweet chocolate** *(far left),* **chopped**

1½ teaspoons **Frangelico** (see Note)

16 **dessert crêpes** (page 113)

4–5 tablespoons (2–2½ oz/ 60–75 g) **unsalted butter**

Confectioners' (icing) sugar for dusting

MANGO MOUSSE WITH RASPBERRY COULIS

FOR THE MOUSSE:

1¼ teaspoons unflavored gelatin

¼ cup (2 fl oz/60 ml) orange or apple juice

1 large mango, peeled and pitted (page 89)

2 large egg whites

¼ teaspoon fresh lemon juice

2 tablespoons superfine (caster) sugar

FOR THE COULIS:

2 cups (8 oz/250 g) raspberries

1½ teaspoons superfine (caster) sugar

1 tablespoon framboise (raspberry liqueur) or Grand Marnier

¼–½ teaspoon fresh lemon juice

Fresh mint sprigs for garnish

To make the mousse, in a small bowl, combine the gelatin with 2 tablespoons cold water to soften. In a saucepan over medium heat, heat the orange juice to just below the boiling point. Remove from the heat, add the gelatin, and stir until it dissolves.

Slice off 4 slivers from the mango and reserve. Cut the remaining mango flesh into cubes. Transfer to a food processor and purée until smooth. Transfer the purée to a glass measuring pitcher; you should have about 1¼ cups (10 fl oz/310 ml). Whisk the gelatin mixture into the purée until blended. Let cool for 10 minutes.

In a large bowl, using an electric mixer on high speed, beat the egg whites until foamy. Add the lemon juice and continue beating until soft peaks form. Gradually add the sugar and continue beating until stiff, glossy peaks form. Using a rubber spatula, fold in the mango mixture. Divide among four 7–fl oz (220-ml) ramekins and smooth the tops. Cover and refrigerate for at least 4 hours or up to overnight.

To make the coulis, in a food processor, combine the raspberries, sugar, and framboise and pulse until smooth. Pass the mixture through a medium-mesh sieve placed over a bowl and stir in ¼ teaspoon of the lemon juice. Taste and add more lemon juice, if needed. Cover and refrigerate until chilled, up to overnight.

Fill a bowl with hot water and dip the base of a ramekin in the water for about 10 seconds. Run a small knife around the inside rim, then invert the mousse onto a plate. Repeat with the remaining mousses. Spoon the coulis onto four plates, top with the mousse, garnish with a mango sliver and mint sprig, and serve.

Note: This recipe contains uncooked egg whites. For information on the risks of uncooked eggs, see page 115.

MAKES 4 SERVINGS

CLEANING RASPBERRIES

Raspberries should not be washed vigorously, as their porous flesh and the hollow center will quickly absorb water, resulting in watery sauces and desserts. If using organic raspberries, you need only brush them gently to remove any debris. Use a soft brush like the ones used for cleaning mushrooms, or a paper towel. If using regular raspberries, wash them briefly under cold running water and drain on paper towels.

FRESH BERRIES WITH ZABAGLIONE

To make the zabaglione, fill a large saucepan with about 2 inches (5 cm) of water and bring to a boil over medium-high heat. Reduce the heat so the water is barely simmering.

In a large copper or stainless-steel bowl, combine the egg yolks and sugar. Using a handheld electric mixer on low speed, beat until smooth, about 30 seconds. Increase the speed to high and beat until the mixture is thick, pale, and fluffy, about 1 minute. Add the Marsala and Cognac to the egg mixture and set the bowl over (but not touching) the simmering water. Reduce the speed to medium and beat for 2 minutes, checking the water frequently to be sure it does not boil. Increase the speed to high and beat until the mixture has tripled in volume and falls in a ribbon when the beaters are lifted, about 3 minutes. Remove the bowl from the pan and whisk the mixture for about 30 seconds. Serve within 5 minutes.

To serve, divide the berries among dessert bowls and spoon the zabaglione on top.

Note: This recipe contains eggs that may be only partially cooked. For more information, see page 115.

MAKES 4 SERVINGS

MARSALA WINE

Named for a Sicilian city in the area where it is made, Marsala, like sherry and Port, is a fortified wine—that is, a wine to which brandy has been added, raising the alcohol content. It was first made in the eighteenth century when an English wine shipper discovered that fortifying the local Sicilian wine prevented it from spoiling on the trip to England. This rich-tasting amber-colored wine is available in sweet and dry. It can be used in sweet and savory recipes, or simply enjoyed as a dessert wine.

FOR THE ZABAGLIONE:

3 large egg yolks

¼ cup (2 oz/60 g) superfine (caster) sugar

⅔ cup (5 fl oz/160 ml) sweet Marsala wine

1 teaspoon Cognac

4 cups (1 lb/500 g) raspberries, blackberries, blueberries, or boysenberries, or a combination

SAUCE BASICS

Whether playing the role of a finishing touch or of an essential component, a sauce should seamlessly complement the dish it accompanies. It should neither overwhelm the other ingredients nor be overshadowed by them. Sauces can be rich, like hollandaise, or light and fresh tasting, like salsa fresca. They can be complex and labor-intensive, like Mexico's mole, or lightning quick to prepare, like a whole-grain mustard pan sauce. In this book you'll find representatives of the classic French tradition, along with some of the best-loved sauces from Cuba, Spain, Argentina, and Thailand.

THE ORIGINS OF SAUCE MAKING

The French may not have created the concept of sauces, but they have elevated sauce making to an art. After the French Revolution, many chefs who had been employed in the kitchens of the aristocracy opened restaurants in Paris and other French cities. They vied with one another for customers, each one attempting to create the most memorable dishes. Sauces were one way to stand out in the crowd.

Béchamel, the classic white sauce made from combining a pale roux of butter and flour with milk and seasonings, was perhaps the first classic French sauce. It had already been in use at least since the reign of Louis XIV, but it gained new prominence in the early years after the Revolution. Many French sauces in those days, however, served two purposes: primarily they added flavor to foods, but were also occasionally used to mask the taste of an ingredient beyond its prime.

MOTHER SAUCES

The "mother" sauces are among the first recipes that students of classic French cooking learn. Each sauce has a number of derivative sauces, so once you have mastered the basic recipes, a large repertory of sauces is available to you.

Hollandaise and mayonnaise are arguably the best known of the sauces thickened with egg yolks. Hollandaise calls for butter and can be transformed into mousseline, with the addition of whipped cream, or maltaise, with the addition of orange juice. Mayonnaise calls for oil rather than butter, and becomes aioli when garlic is mixed in, or rémoulade when capers, mustard, parsley, and other seasonings are added.

For béarnaise sauce, yet another mother sauce, butter is beaten into a reduction of vinegar or lemon juice, and the mixture is thickened with egg yolks over heat. Finally, *sauce espagnole*, the traditional brown sauce of the French kitchen, goes into the making of demi-glace as well as bordelaise sauce, which also includes bone marrow.

INTERNATIONAL SAUCES

The world of sauces, of course, reaches far beyond the borders of France. In Latin American countries, for example, where table sauces are commonly called salsas or *mojos,* many of them are made from fruits, vegetables, and herbs, and butter is rarely used. In India, curry sauces vary from one end of the country to the other and typically combine a large number of spices, while in Italy, every region has its own pasta sauces, whether it is the pesto of Liguria, the *ragù* of Emilia-Romagna, or the amatriciana of Lazio. Some Italian sauces use butter and cream, such as the Alfredo sauce that coats fettuccine, but many sauces—particularly those in the Italian south—call for olive oil.

Vegetables, primarily tomatoes, rather than flour or egg yolks, are what generally give Italian sauces their body. Nuts are yet another means of giving body to a sauce. Smooth and thick Mexican mole calls for almonds—and dozens of other ingredients—while coconut milk–rich Thai peanut sauce is thickened with finely ground nuts. Finally, body is sometimes delivered by simply whisking in oil, as in the herb-and-spice-laced *charmoula* of Morocco.

ESSENTIAL TECHNIQUES

The goal in making most sauces is to thicken a flavorful liquid so that it coats the main ingredients in a pleasing way. If a sauce is too thin, it will run off onto the plate and the dish will not benefit from the flavor that the sauce was intended to provide. Conversely, if the sauce is too thick, it will be neither pleasing to the eye nor tempting to the palate. Several techniques are used to infuse liquids with flavor and to thicken them to the desired consistency.

DEGLAZING

When fish, poultry, or meat is sautéed or roasted in a pan with butter or oil, a caramelizing process takes place.

As the ingredients sizzle in the pan, a "fond," a coating of crisp, flavorful bits, forms on the bottom of the pan. In order to transfer this flavor into the pan sauce, a liquid—usually wine, often mixed with a stock and sometimes water or fruit juice—is added to the sizzling pan after the main ingredient has been removed. "Deglazing," stirring and simmering this liquid, softens the fond and distributes it throughout the liquid. Deglazing is an essential step in making almost any pan sauce.

EMULSIFYING

When creating an emulsion, two liquids that tend to remain separate—such as oil and water—are coaxed into forming one thickened, opaque liquid with the help of an emulsifier such as egg yolk or mustard. Mustard is an easy emulsifier to use, and it often helps to hold together oil and vinegar emulsions like vinaigrettes. These tenuous emulsions usually separate after a few minutes, but can quickly be whisked back into their creamy state.

Hot emulsions such as béarnaise and sabayon are the trickiest to make. Do not use eggs that have been frozen or pasteurized, as they may separate and are less likely to create a successful emulsion.

Shown opposite are the basic steps in making an egg-based emulsion, in this case, hollandaise sauce.

1 Melting the butter: In a small saucepan over low heat, melt the butter. Remove from the heat and place in a heatproof measuring cup. Place 2 ice cubes in a small bowl near the stove.

2 Whisking the egg yolks: In another small saucepan, combine the water, egg yolks, and salt. Place over low heat and immediately begin whisking. Whisking all the time, keep the pan over the heat until the mixture begins to steam and thickens slightly to the consistency of a thin yogurt. This will take 1–3 minutes.

3 Preventing graininess: If the yolk mixture begins to look even slightly grainy, remove the pan from the heat and add the ice cube. Whisk vigorously until the ice melts and the mixture returns to a smooth, mayonnaise-like consistency.

4 Finishing the sauce: Begin adding the butter a small amount at a time, moving the pan on and off of the heat to keep the mixture lukewarm (warm enough to keep the butter liquid, but not so hot that the yolks begin to curdle). If the yolks do begin to curdle, again whisk in an ice cube off the heat. Keep adding the butter about a tablespoon at a time, whisking, until all the butter is added and the sauce is smooth.

PLATING SAUCES

For the most attractive presentation of sauces like béarnaise and crème anglaise, spoon a little sauce onto a plate and tip the plate to spread the sauce into a thin, even layer (or use the back of a spoon). Pan sauces are usually drizzled over the top of a main dish, while salsas and relishes look best in a neat mound or, if liquidy, in a small bowl or ramekin.

STORING SAUCES

Most sauces are highly perishable. Salsas will quickly discolor, and hot emulsions solidify when cooled and cannot be rewarmed without breaking. Tomato-based pasta sauces and chocolate sauces that do not contain cream, as well as mole sauce, may be refrigerated for up to 5 days. A good rule of thumb: any sauce that contains eggs or cream should not be kept for more than 2 days.

PASTA SAUCE BASICS

Some pasta sauces are based on tomatoes, either puréed or simply diced and cooked until almost liquefied. Others, mainly from northern Italy, are based around cream, cheese, or butter. Some pasta sauces are hardly sauces at all in the conventional sense, but rather an amalgamation of dry ingredients—usually vegetables and herbs, such as pesto—which coats and flavors the pasta. This last type in particular, because it lacks liquid, is often helped by the addition of a small amount of the pasta cooking water. The cooking water contains starches and nutrients, and thins and extends the sauce, while also helping it to adhere to the pasta. Simply reserve about ¼ cup (2 fl oz/60 ml) of the water just before draining the pasta, and either add it to the sauce itself, or add it to the bowl of pasta and sauce once they have been combined.

To further infuse the pasta with the flavor of the sauce, make the sauce in a frying pan large enough to hold all the pasta as well, and, after draining the pasta, turn the pasta into the pan of sauce. Cook gently, stirring and tossing for a couple of minutes before serving. The sauce will thicken slightly and glaze each piece of pasta.

DESSERT SAUCE BASICS

Imagine a dish of vanilla ice cream. Now imagine it covered in luscious hot fudge sauce. A sweet sauce can transform a simple dish into a sensual experience.

WORKING WITH CHOCOLATE

Chocolate is usually melted for cooking, which must be done carefully, as it scorches easily. The best way to melt chocolate is to chop it and then place it in the top pan of a double boiler set over barely simmering water in the bottom pan. The water must not touch the top pan and it must not boil. If steam begins to rise and comes in contact with the chocolate, the chocolate may seize, or harden. Make sure to stir the chocolate occasionally as it melts, and remove the top pan from over the simmering water once the chocolate is fully melted.

Chocolate can also be melted in a microwave oven. Again, chop it, then place it in a microwave-safe dish and heat it on the lowest setting, stopping to stir it every 15 to 20 seconds.

MAKING A CUSTARD SAUCE

Temperature is also the most important factor in custard making. When you add egg yolks or whole eggs to hot milk or cream, they must be "tempered" first by whisking in a little of the hot liquid to warm them up; otherwise they may curdle. Once the eggs and milk are combined, do not allow the mixture to rise above 170°F/77°C (use an instant-read thermometer to test), or the eggs may curdle. Custard cooked at a lower temperature for a longer period of time is less likely to curdle.

TOOLS FOR SAUCES

Many sauces can be made with the most basic kitchen tools: sharp knives, a good pan, a whisk, a wooden spoon. But in some cases, making a sauce becomes easier if you have the right specialized tool for the task.

PANS

A good collection of saucepans in various sizes is imperative for sauce making. Cooking a sauce in a pan with a thin base will lead to scorching, while low-heat simmering—crucial for reduction sauces like bordelaise—is virtually impossible in such a pan. Your saucepans should have smooth, heavy bases, which reduce the possibility of scorching and ensure even heat distribution. The handles should be solidly attached and placed so that lifting and pouring is easily managed. High-quality pans are usually expensive, however, so if you are not already well outfitted, be prepared to spend some money.

MORTAR AND PESTLE

Serious sauce makers will want to start off their aioli and pesto and grind their own spices in this ancient tool. Buy a large one to avoid having to switch to a bowl to finish the sauce. Marble is the best material, as it does not absorb any food odors and it stands up to the pounding of the pestle. A large, heavy ceramic mortar is also a good choice.

KNIVES

For making some salsas and *mojos* and *chimichurri*, a razor-sharp chef's knife is imperative. Fine chopping with a knife is preferred over chopping in a food processor for these sauces because the individual ingredients should remain distinct, rather than blend together. Look for a chef's knife with a blade made of a carbon–stainless-steel alloy; it will sharpen easily and will keep its edge.

FOOD PROCESSOR AND BLENDER

These two pieces of equipment are good for different tasks, and the serious cook will want to have both of them. Food processors are best for chopping, and thus are invaluable for making *romesco* sauce, salsa verde, and raspberry coulis. Blenders pulverize and make the best moles, vinaigrettes, and fruit sauces. Mayonnaise can be made successfully in either a food processor or blender.

A mini processor is useful for making smaller amounts of sauce and for grinding some ingredients for sauces. Some blenders come with small jars, in addition to the standard beaker, that can be used in the same way. Make sure that your blender beaker has a tight-fitting lid, as sauces sometimes threaten to overflow when blending at high speed.

WHISKS

Also known as whips, whisks are indispensable for sauce making. You will need three basic types, a balloon whisk, a so-called sauce whisk, and a nonstick whisk.

Balloon whisks, sometimes called egg whisks, taper to a bulb shape and have springy wires, making them ideal for whipping egg whites to stiff peaks. Generally, the more wires, the more efficient the whipping, although the whisk will also be heavier, and thus more tiring to use.

Sauce whisks have a more slender profile and the wires are more closely set and rigid. They are excellent for mixing a vinaigrette, whipping up a mayonnaise, or whisking in butter to finish a sauce. Some sauce whisks have flat heads and fewer wires and are good for blending ingredients while aerating the mixture slightly.

Nonstick whisks are simply whisks made of heatproof plastic, so they can safely be used when cooking with nonstick pans without scraping up the finish.

BASIC RECIPES

The recipes that follow are referred to often in this book.

CHICKEN STOCK

6 lb (3 kg) chicken necks and backs

3 celery stalks

3 carrots, peeled

2 yellow onions, halved

2 leeks, white and light green parts only, sliced

4 fresh flat-leaf (Italian) parsley sprigs

1 fresh thyme sprig

1 bay leaf

Salt and freshly ground pepper

Combine the chicken parts, celery, carrots, onions, leeks, parsley, thyme, and bay leaf in a large stockpot. Add water just to cover the ingredients. Slowly bring to a boil over medium heat. Reduce the heat to as low as possible and let simmer, uncovered, for 3 hours, regularly skimming off the foam that rises to the surface. Taste and season with salt and pepper.

Strain the stock into a bowl through a colander or sieve lined with cheesecloth (muslin). Let cool at room temperature for about 1 hour, then cover and refrigerate for at least 30 minutes or up to overnight. With a large spoon, remove the hardened fat from the surface and discard it.

Cover and refrigerate the stock for up to 3 days, or pour into airtight containers or zippered plastic freezer bags and freeze for up to 3 months. Makes about 3 qt (3 l).

BEEF STOCK

4 lb (2 kg) beef bones, with some meat attached

4 fresh flat-leaf (Italian) parsley sprigs

1 fresh thyme sprig

1 bay leaf

2 large carrots, peeled and cut into 2-inch (5-cm) slices

1 large onion, cut into 2-inch (5-cm) slices

2 leeks, light green and dark green parts only, sliced into 2-inch (5-cm) chunks

Preheat the oven to 425°F (220°C). Place the beef bones in a large roasting pan. Place in the oven and roast until browned, about 1½ hours, stirring a few times to give the bones an even color.

Wrap the parsley, thyme, and bay leaf in cheesecloth (muslin) and secure the bundle with kitchen string to make a bouquet garni.

Remove the pan from the oven. Transfer the bones to a large stockpot. Add about 3 cups (24 fl oz/ 750 ml) water to the roasting pan and place it over medium-high heat. Bring to a boil and deglaze the pan, stirring to scrape the browned bits from the pan's bottom. The water will become a rich brown color.

Transfer the deglazed juices from the roasting pan to the stockpot and add enough cold water (about 3.5 qt/3.5 l) to just cover the bones. Add the carrots, onion, leeks, and the bouquet garni.

Bring to a boil over medium heat, then reduce the heat to low. Let simmer, uncovered, for 4 hours, using a spoon or skimmer to regularly skim off the foam that rises to the surface. Taste and adjust the seasoning.

Turn off the heat and let the stock cool for ½ hour. Remove the bones and pour the stock into a large bowl through a fine-meshed strainer lined with cheesecloth (muslin). Let cool to room temperature, then cover and refrigerate for 2 hours.

With a large spoon, remove the hardened fat from the surface and discard it. Pour into containers and refrigerate. The stock will keep for up to 3 days in the refrigerator or 3 months in the freezer. Makes 3 qt (3 l).

DESSERT CRÊPES

1 cup (5 oz/155 g) all-purpose (plain) flour

2 tablespoons sugar

¼ teaspoon salt

1 cup (8 fl oz/250 ml) whole milk, at room temperature

6 tablespoons (3 oz/90 g) unsalted butter, melted

3 large eggs, at room temperature

In a food processor, combine the flour, sugar, and salt and pulse briefly to blend. In a glass measuring pitcher, combine the milk, butter, and eggs. With the motor running, pour in the milk mixture and purée until very smooth. Cover and refrigerate the batter for 1 hour, then pour into a glass measuring pitcher. The batter should be a little thicker than heavy (double) cream; if it is too thick, whisk in 1–2 teaspoons water.

Set an 8- or 9-inch (20- or 23-cm) nonstick frying pan over medium heat. Ladle in ¼ cup (2 fl oz/60 ml) of the batter. Immediately swirl the pan to cover the bottom evenly; the crêpe should be very thin. Cook until the top of the crêpe is firm and has lost its sheen and the edges have just begun to turn golden, 30–40 seconds. Flip the crêpe over with a rubber spatula and cook for 20 seconds more until firm and slightly golden. Transfer to a plate. Reduce the heat to medium-low and repeat. Cover the cooled crêpes with plastic wrap and set aside until ready to serve. Makes 16 crêpes.

FRESH PAPPARDELLE PASTA

2 cups (10 oz/315 g) all-purpose (plain) flour, plus more for kneading

4 large eggs, at room temperature

1 tablespoon extra-virgin olive oil

Put the flour in a food processor. In a glass measuring pitcher, whisk together the eggs and olive oil. With the motor running, slowly add about three-fourths of the egg mixture, pulsing on and off until a stiff dough forms. Add the remaining egg mixture only if the dough does not come together quickly.

Turn the dough out onto a floured surface and knead using the ball of your hand for 15 minutes (the dough will be stiff). Shape the dough into a cylinder and wrap tightly in plastic wrap. Let stand at room temperature for 30 minutes or up to 2 hours.

Cut the dough into 6 equal pieces. Keep the dough you are not immediately working with covered with a kitchen towel. Using a hand-cranked pasta machine, roll 1 piece of the dough through the widest setting on the machine. Fold the dough in half lengthwise and pass it through the rollers again. Dust the dough lightly with flour only if it begins to stick to the rollers. Adjust the rollers to the next-narrower setting, fold the dough in half, and pass it through the rollers. Repeat this twice, again dusting with flour as needed. The dough will be getting longer and thinner with each pass. Fold the dough and pass it through each progressively narrower setting, again dusting with flour as needed and stopping at the next to last setting. The dough sheet should be long and smooth and thin enough to see the shadow of your hand through it.

Gently place the pasta sheet on a wooden drying rack or a dry wooden cutting board. Repeat with the remaining dough; do not stack the sheets.

After each sheet of dough has dried for about 10 minutes (it should still be slightly pliable and not yet cracking), use a large knife to cut into strips 1¼ inches (3 cm) wide by 4 inches (10 cm) long. Cover with a kitchen towel to prevent the pasta from drying out.

Cook immediately, or place on a lightly floured baking sheet, wrap tightly in plastic wrap, and refrigerate for up to 3 days. Makes about 1¼ lb (625 g).

GLOSSARY

ALMONDS, GROUND To grind almonds, freeze slivered almonds for 30 minutes, transfer to a food processor, and, pulsing the machine on and off, process to a fine meal; the texture should resemble dry bread crumbs. Do not overprocess or you will end up with almond butter.

ASPARAGUS, PEELING To prepare asparagus for cooking, first remove the woody ends, cutting them off with a knife or by gently bending the stalk about 2 inches (5 cm) from the end. The stalk should snap naturally, right at the point where the tender and tough parts meet. Using a vegetable peeler, scrape the thin outer layer of peel from an inch or two below the tip's leaf buds to the end of the stalk. If using the freshest slender springtime asparagus, peeling should not be necessary.

BALSAMIC VINEGAR The distinctive sweet-sour flavor of balsamic vinegar has become highly popular. True balsamic vinegar, called *aceto balsamico tradizionale*, is expensive and hard to find. For cooking, a good-quality balsamic vinegar made from wine vinegar flavored with a small percentage of *mosto cotto*, or "cooked must," is just fine. Check the label carefully before you buy, as many inexpensive balsamic vinegars are wine vinegars sweetened and darkened with caramel coloring.

CHILES, FRESH Here are a few very common chile types used in the recipes in this book.

Chipotle: The smoked and dried version of jalapeños, chipotles are widely available canned with garlic, tomatoes, and vinegar and labeled "*chiles chipotles en adobo.*" They are moderately hot and have a distinctively smoky flavor

Jalapeño: This bright green chile ranges from hot to very hot. It is available fresh or canned and is sometimes seen in its bright red, ripe state.

Serrano: This small, slender, shiny chile is very hot. The green type is most commonly available. Dried serranos are occasionally available as well.

Poblano: This stocky chile is about 5 inches (13 cm) long, 3 inches (7.5 cm) in diameter, and medium-hot. The most common poblano is dark green, shading to almost black in some spots; deep red poblanos are less common. When dried, the poblano is known as an ancho.

CHILES, HANDLING All chiles contain capsaicin, a compound that gives them their heat and can irritate your skin and other sensitive areas. Wear gloves to protect your hands, and when you have finished working with chiles, thoroughly wash your hands and any tools you have used with hot, soapy water. See page 24 for more on handling chiles.

CHIVES These long, thin, dark green members of the onion family taste like a more delicate and sweet green (spring) onion, and are often used as a garnish on sauces or soups. Using a chef's knife, cut them into pieces about ⅛ inch (3 mm) long, rather than mincing them. Some cooks use a pair of kitchen scissors to snip the chives, which is easier than chopping them.

CITRUS, ZESTING The zest is the colored, outer part of a citrus peel, where most of the flavorful oils are concentrated. The white part of the peel, or pith, is bitter. Recipes that call for chopped or grated peel generally mean only the zest, which can be removed in a number of ways. You can use a zester, a tool with small, sharp holes at the end of a stainless steel blade that you pull across the peel, removing the zest in thin strips. You can also use a vegetable peeler or paring knife to remove the zest in wider strips, which can then be chopped or minced, or you can grate the zest on the fine rasps on a handheld grater-shredder or on a Microplane grater.

DOUBLE BOILER Used for gentle cooking, warming, or melting, a double boiler is made up of two pots, one nesting on top of the other, with one lid that fits both pots. A small amount of water is brought to a simmer in the bottom pan, while ingredients are placed in the top pan to heat gently. The food is warmed by the heat of the steam from below. A double boiler is used when direct heat could scorch or curdle delicate ingredients, such as when melting chocolate or making egg-based sauces.

EGGS, SAFETY Eggs are sometimes used raw or partially cooked in this book. These eggs run the risk of being infected with salmonella or other bacteria, which can lead to food poisoning. This risk is of the most serious concern to small children, older people, pregnant women, and anyone with a compromised immune system. If you have health and safety concerns, do not eat raw eggs.

EGGS, TEMPERING When making custard, you must handle the eggs carefully. If eggs are heated up very quickly and suddenly, they will curdle, resulting in a texture very similar to that of scrambled eggs. For a silky custard texture, the eggs must be tempered, or heated gradually. A splash of hot liquid is stirred into the eggs before they are poured into a hot pan on the stove top. Constant stirring as the eggs heat also helps keep the process slow and gradual.

GRANA PADANO This is a high-quality aged cow's cheese, similar to Parmigiano-Reggiano and made in the Po Valley of northern Italy. It generally has a yellower cast than Parmesan, and can generally be substituted in any recipe that calls for Parmesan (or other aged grating cheese).

MANDOLINE This narrow, rectangular tool, usually made of stainless steel, is used for slicing and julienning. It sits at an angle on the work surface, and the food to be cut is slid over a mounted blade. Some mandolines come with an assortment of blades that will produce a variety of shapes and thicknesses. This handy tool simplifies the task of creating thin, uniform slices.

PARMESAN Parmesan cheese is a firm, aged, salty cheese made from cow's milk. True Parmesan cheese comes from the Emilia-Romagna region of northern Italy and is referred to by its trademark name, Parmigiano-Reggiano. Rich and complex in flavor and often possessing a pleasant granular texture, this savory cheese is best when grated only as needed just before use in a recipe or at the table.

PASTA Many cooks may think that all dried pastas are alike, but in fact quality varies. For best results, look for brands imported from Italy. When cooking pasta, always use a large pot and fill it two-thirds to three-fourths full of water. When the water is at a rapid boil, add 1 tablespoon kosher salt for each 4 quarts (2 l) of water and then add the pasta. There is no need to add oil to the water, as some recipes suggest. As soon as the pasta is in the pot, stir it to keep it from sticking together and then continue to stir occasionally as it cooks. Cook according to the package instructions until the pasta it is al dente—tender but still slightly firm to the bite.

Drain the pasta in a colander and shake briefly to remove excess water, but do not rinse it.

SEA SALT This type of salt, created by natural evaporation, is available in coarse or fine grains that are shaped like hollow, flaky pyramids. Due to its shape, it adheres better to foods and dissolves more quickly than table salt. Sea salt from France, England, and the United States is available in specialty stores and well-stocked supermarkets. The most prized sea salt is the grayish-ivory *fleur de sel* from Brittany.

SEMOLINA FLOUR This somewhat coarse flour is milled from durum wheat, a variety that is particularly high in protein. The flour is almost always used in the manufacture of dried pastas. It is also used in some pizza doughs and breads.

SUPERFINE SUGAR Finely ground granulated sugar, also known as caster or castor sugar, dissolves more quickly than regular sugar and is therefore a good choice when sugar is to be mixed in with water or other cold ingredients.

VERMOUTH A fortified wine flavored with various spices, herbs, and fruits, vermouth is available in two basic styles: sweet (also known as Italian or red) and dry. Dry vermouth, an ingredient in the classic martini, is also used in cooking, and is especially good when making a pan sauce.

INDEX

SIMON & SCHUSTER SOURCE
A division of Simon & Schuster, Inc.
Rockefeller Center
1230 Avenue of the Americas
New York, NY 10020

WILLIAMS-SONOMA
Founder and Vice-Chairman: Chuck Williams

WELDON OWEN INC.
Chief Executive Officer: John Owen
President and Chief Operating Officer: Terry Newell
Vice President, International Sales: Stuart Laurence
Creative Director: Gaye Allen
Series Editor: Sarah Putman Clegg
Editor: Emily Miller
Designer: Leon Yu
Design Assistant: Marisa Kwek
Production Director: Chris Hemesath
Color Manager: Teri Bell
Shipping and Production Coordinator: Todd Rechner

Weldon Owen wishes to thank the following for their
generous assistance: Copy Editors Kris Balloun and
Sharron Wood; Contributing Editor Sharon Silva; Food
and Prop Stylists Kim Konecny and Erin Quon; Assistant
Food Stylists Lori Nunokawa and Sharon Ardiana;
Photographer's Assistant Selena Aument; Proofreaders
Desne Ahlers and Carrie Bradley; Contributing Writer
Kate Chynoweth; Indexer Ken DellaPenta.

Set in Trajan, Utopia, and Vectora.

Williams-Sonoma Collection *Sauce* was
conceived and produced by Weldon Owen Inc.,
814 Montgomery Street, San Francisco,
California 94133, in collaboration with
Williams-Sonoma, 3250 Van Ness Avenue,
San Francisco, California 94109.

A Weldon Owen Production
Copyright © 2004 by Weldon Owen Inc. and
Williams-Sonoma, Inc.

For information regarding special discounts for
bulk purchases, please contact Simon & Schuster
Special Sales at 1-800-456-6798 or
business@simonandschuster.com

Color separations by Bright Arts Graphics
Singapore (Pte.) Ltd.
Printed and bound in Singapore by Tien Wah
Press (Pte.) Ltd.

First printed in 2004.

10 9 8 7 6 5 4

Library of Congress Cataloging-in-Publication
data is available.

ISBN 0-7432-6187-9

A NOTE ON WEIGHTS AND MEASURES

All recipes include customary U.S. and metric measurements. Metric conversions are based on
a standard developed for these books and have been rounded off. Actual weights may vary.